Rental Property

How to Buy, Rehab, Rent, Re-finance, and Manage.

By

Jvandomi

© COPYRIGHT 2019 by Jvandomi

All rights reserved.

This record is outfitted towards furnishing accurate and reliable data concerning the point and issue secured. The production is sold with the possibility that the distributor isn't required to render bookkeeping, authoritatively allowed, or something else, qualified administrations. On the off chance that counsel is essential, legitimate, or proficient, a rehearsed individual in the calling ought to be requested.

- From a Declaration of Principles, which was acknowledged and affirmed similarly by a Committee of the American Bar Association and a Committee of Distributors and Associations.

Not the slightest bit is it lawful to repeat, copy, or transmit any piece of this record in either electronic methods or printed design. Recording of

this production is carefully precluded, and any the capacity of this report isn't permitted except if with composed authorization from the distributor. All rights held.

The data gave in this is expressed, to be honest, and predictable, in that any obligation, as far as heedlessness or something else, by any utilization or maltreatment of any approaches, procedures, or bearings contained inside is the singular and articulate duty of the Beneficiary peruse. By no means will any legitimate obligation or fault be held against the distributor for any reparation harms, or fiscal misfortune because of the data in this, either straightforwardly or in a roundabout way. Individual creators possess all copyrights not held by the distributor.

The data thus is offered for instructive Purposes exclusively and is all-inclusive as so. The introduction of the information is without an agreement or on the other hand, any assurance affirmation.

The trademarks that are utilized are with no consent, and the production of the trademark is without authorization or support by the trademark proprietor. All trademarks and brands inside this book

are for explaining purposes and are claimed by the proprietors themselves, not subsidiary with this report

Introduction

In this book, I want to motivate and educate you. I want to get you started in real estate. I plan to induce you that rental property can, in any case, lead you to a lifetime of riches and individual satisfaction.

Regardless of what monetary objectives you set for yourself, regardless of how little money, credit, or salary you as of now have, in the event that you decide to, you can, in any case, construct your fortune in real estate.

Regardless of whether you own solitary family home, a duplex, a triplex, or numerous units, if you lease it out, you're a landlord. What's more, as a landlord, you need great knowledge. This book starts with the fundamentals and takes you through a wide range of strides along the way.

In all honesty, numerous people who buy and manage their very own investment properties appreciate it. Along these lines, in the end, you may build up your management business and start to manage other people's properties, notwithstanding your own properties. Whatever your conditions, you must comprehend the rudiments of property management. This book answers huge numbers of your most pressing inquiries on rental property.

Table of Contents

Introduction 4
The Housing Market 7
The benefit of Investing in Real Estate 9
The Risk of Investing in Rentals 12
    Paths to Building Wealth with Real Estate 15
Purchase Below Market Value 22
Create Value with Property Improvements 23
    Different Ways to Improve 23
Shield Your Profits from the IRS (Tax Shelter) 26
How to Determine a Good Property 29
How to Choose the Right Location 31
Selecting the Right Type of House 33
How to Secure a Great Deal on Real Estate 42
    Places to get Rental Houses 42
Purchasing Rental Property 52
    Ways of acquiring property 52
    Tips for Purchasing an Investment Property . 57
    Methods of Structuring a Purchase 62
How to Invest in Rentals with less Cash and Bad Credit 67
How to Analyze an Area for Rental 74
How to Analyze the Market 78
Offer and Negotiations 81
    Negotiating for the Best Price and Terms 81

- Steps to Successful Negotiations.................81
- How to Manage and Keep Your Property...................91
- Building Your Team 97
- Taxes, Licenses, and Insurance 104
  - Types of taxes..105
  - Depreciation...108
  - Business licenses and permits...................110
  - Types of insurance......................................112
- Exit Strategy..116
  - What Is A Business Exit Strategy? 116
  - What Is A Real Estate Exit Strategy? 117
  - How to Choose the Right Exit Strategy 118
- The Importance of Record Keeping 125

The Housing Market

Purchasing, managing, and selling real estate can be one of the most beneficial and compensating venture activities you can partake in. There is the same number of approaches to put resources into real estate as there are individuals. Most speculation systems focus on different time skylines. Though a few investors, for instance, want to adopt a momentary approach by "flipping" or "rehabbing" houses, different investors like to adopt a long-term approach that incorporates purchasing, managing, and holding investment properties for quite a while. Volume is a critical factor that influences the two procedures. For example, broaden the volume of units purchased and sold, or flipped, builds the investor's opportunity to create benefits. By a similar token, expanding the volume of units purchased oversaw, and held in a portfolio builds the investor's opportunity to create pay. This book is expected for people who, as of now, believe themselves to be smart in their approach to investing in real estate, just as for the individuals who want to become smart in their approach to investing in real estate.

The housing business sector has performed very well generally. When contrasted and other asset classes, for example, stocks or commodities, it has been considerably more unsurprising and not so unpredictable. While there have been some level long periods of expanding home values and even some declining years, home values, by and large, have risen quite a long time after year. As per the U.S. Enumeration Bureau, new home costs have ascended from the cost of a normal deal of $19,300 in 1963 to $228,300 in 2002.

This is a complete increment in the value of 1082.9 percent over a 40-year time frame, which speaks to an entirely decent annualized development pace of 6.37 percent. Hence, if you were blessed enough to procure a little arrangement of just five investment properties in 1963, their total value today would be worth, all things considered, a lot.

The benefit of Investing in Real Estate.

The historical performance of real estate as an asset class catches just one segment of the additions accessible to investors and results from an increase in worth that can be credited to price appreciation. There are three extra ways inalienable in real estate on which investors can underwrite, also. Advantages accumulate through decreases in the head of an advance, through duty investment funds, and net positive salary produced from rents.

Changes in real estate esteem that accelerate through appreciation, or increases in price, basically are because of two variables—increases in the money supply and increases in demand. The Federal Reserve Board (Fed) is answerable for changes in the nation's supply of money. Increases in the money supply result in the downgrading of the dollar and, then again, cause prices to increase, or blow up. As more dollars enter the market and become accessible to buy products, they start to decrease in worth.

In addition to the fact that it cost less to get into the films, yet the expenses of nourishment, fuel, and housing, just as every other great, additionally were substantially less at that point. The ensuing ascent in prices is a result of increases in the supply of money, also called swelling. The second part of price appreciation reflects changes in the demand for housing. Positive changes in monetary conditions for some families in the course of the most recent couple of decades have made the probability of home proprietorship a reality along these lines increasing in demand. Other huge variables that have added to the demand for housing are the development in the nation's populace from two essential sources. The first happens normally through the introduction of kids, while the second comes from a relentless flow of settlers into the nation.

The second benefit to owners of investment in rental property gathers through decreases in loan principal. Every month as the home loan payment is made, a bit of the payment is applied to both the interest and the principal. Since diminishing the principal means lessening the loan balance, as the payments are made without fail and consistently, the balance, in the long run, will be forked over the required funds. In the early years of repayment, the greater part of the payment is applied to the enthusiasm, with next to no being applied to the principal. After some time, be that as it may, the individual extents start to invert slowly as the intriguing bit diminishes, and the principal bit increments. A loan with a thirty-year amortization period, for instance, will be squared away totally in precisely 360 months if equivalent payments are made over the length of the loan. The excellence of this benefit is that the inhabitants are making the monthly payments and, in this way, diminishing the loan balance.

The third benefit to proprietors of venture rental property is gotten from a decrease in their tax liability. The Internal Revenue Service (IRS) orders that rental property be devalued over a time skyline. Deterioration can be a touch of befuddling to investors who are new to the idea. The significant thing to comprehend is that it is a count made fundamentally for tax purposes and doesn't matter to the cash flow from activities. The figurine is made for personal tax revealing purposes and ought not to be viewed as when assessing the cash flow from a rental property since this is a yearly occasion and can't be applied adequately to progressing monthly expenses. Beyond reasonable doubt, however, a decrease in one's tax liability is an undeniable benefit, and relying upon what number of properties are possessed, and the productivity of everyone, an investor's tax liability can be diminished to zero.

The fourth benefit to proprietors of speculation rental property emerges from the net positive cash flow created from the monthly payments made by the inhabitant. It is the segment staying after taking the distinction of the monthly rental pay less all expenses. Investors of rental houses ought to endeavor to buy just properties that meet two tests. The principal test is to find a rental property that is estimated at or beneath honest worth, and the subsequent test is to ensure that the property cash flows appropriately.

For a rental property's cash to flow appropriately, it ought to be adequate to create a lingering on a proceeding with the premise. This implies toward the day's end, after all, expenses for the month have been paid, including principal, interest, taxes, and protection (PITI), an investor ought to have something left finished. A net positive monetary flow from the property is only one more way investor can benefit by owning rental properties.

The Risk of Investing in Rentals

Most would contend that the risks of owning rental properties are genuinely self-evident, yet you'd be astounded what number of people ask me what they are. If you are brand new to land contributing, it will bode well that you may not comprehend the risks in a manner that considers a greater picture see. This is essential because of them that you don't realize what variables to look at. Or on the other hand, regardless of whether you aren't brand new, at times, it's only useful to see a general outline of things as an approach to help drill it in and help you better get it.

Before discussing the risks, one thing you need to be extremely clear about with regards to rental properties is the numbers. I didn't have the foggiest idea about a thing about how to run numbers on a forthcoming rental property when I initially got interested in real estate, and I've since discovered that a great many people truly don't have an idea about them. In all actuality: Most properties don't make great rental property ventures! I typically hear it's in about the 80% territory that properties don't work out monetarily as rental properties. Why would that be? Since the numbers don't work. I'm not catching my meaning, "the numbers don't work"? It implies that your real costs (which are typically more than what people acknowledge) surpass the pay on the property, and along these lines, you lose cash. Losing cash isn't the purpose of contributing. Making cash is.

<u>*Vacancy*</u>

This one is somewhat of a trickster since it's not as evident as probably the remainder of the risk factors. Be that as it may, despite being a trickster, it tends to be one of the most expensive issues with an investment property! Different issues can be expensive too. However, vacancies can happen regularly and rapidly on the off chance that you aren't cautious. The costs related with vacancies are: lost rental salary during every month of opening (particularly noteworthy on the off chance that you need to pay a home loan installment every month simultaneously), turnover-actuated fixes, and on the off chance that you are utilizing an agent to verify inhabitants, you should quite not too bad lump to that agent once they spot occupants (typically what could be compared to one month's lease). For reasons unknown, when some people originally began purchasing investment properties, they genuinely belittled the intensity of opportunity costs. It is unknown whether they thought vacancies wouldn't happen or if they didn't understand to what extent vacancies could last. It is safe to say that certainly, they didn't place enough weight on them. Pay attention to them — because they are very important.

Damage/Repairs/Maintenance

This class could be simply called "when you need to fix something." There are a couple of reasons you may need to fix something on your investment property. There could have been robbery or occupant actuated harm. There could be simply ordinary fixes, either from typical consistently wear or little things that will in general break. Or then again, there could be more Cap Ex-level maintenance. This could incorporate things like rooftops and water warmers, or it tends to be progressively difficult issues, as basic issues, inward wiring, or something that you might have thought about when you purchased the property. Fixing things can run everywhere for the expense. Minor fixes could be under $100, significant fixes could hit a huge number of dollars, and there is each cost plausibility in the middle. The genuine success happens when greater things are secured by protection. Be that as it may, you can't ever rely on the protection wins, so consistently accept the cost will be out of your pocket and plan appropriately.

Decreased Rents

This one isn't exactly as evident as vacancies and repairs. What you are taking a gander at here is how a lot of the property is getting in rental income. This is important since, well, the amount it gets is extremely the core of the benefits since you need enough cash coming in to cover the amount of cash going out — your expenses. So, when does this become a risk? The risk comes in situations where monetary states of the market change with the end goal that you can never again get as high of rental income as you once could. On the off chance that general rents decline, and hence you need to diminish how a lot of leases you request on your property to remain aggressive, all of a sudden, you could have an income level that doesn't bolster the cost degree of the property. Bode well? Or then again perhaps the monetary conditions don't change by any stretch of the imagination, and for reasons unknown, you were only ready to charge a specific tenant a truly elevated lease, yet then when that tenant leaves, you can't locate another tenant who will pay that much. The key here is continually having rents that outperform what you are paying in expenses. Rents being constrained down is a risk for rental property proprietors.

Decreased Property Value

Presently, I need to be clear about what I mean by the estimation of the property is a hazard factor. The estimation of a property doesn't make a difference except if you are buying or selling it (or refinancing it). Did you hear that? Give me a chance to state it once more. The estimation of a property doesn't make a difference except if you are buying or selling it (or refinancing it). So, when I state that property estimation can be a risk, it just must be in extraordinary conditions. The one outrageous situation that I can consider is the point at which the market the property is in decreases so that you can never again gather sufficiently high rents (or any rents) to cover your costs, so you are missing out each month (possibly quickly), and the main decision is to sell, however the incentive on the property has failed. At that point what? All things considered, that is bad. Except if that situation occurs. However, you don't need to stress a lot over the worth.

Paths to Building Wealth with Real Estate

Multiple Paths to Building Wealth Now, you're going to see why real estate investing offers you greater opportunities to build wealth than any other type of investment.

You can make money in a different number of ways with real estate. For starters, here are potential paths to profit:

- Appreciation in market values
- Condominium conversions
- Inflation
- Improved management
- Cash flows
- More-profitable market strategy
- Mortgage payoff
- Tax shelter

- Buy below market
- Discounted notes and tax deeds
- Create property value
- Real estate stocks (REITs, home builders, mortgage lenders)
- Create site value

Appreciation in Market

Qualities over time of 5 to 10 years, almost a wide range of properties gain in worth since population, occupations, incomes, and riches (buying influence) become quicker than the measure of new development. Over the long haul, more people with more cash reliably push land costs up. "OK," you counter, "however, that was at that point, and this is currently. Costs can't continue to increase as they have previously?" be that as it may, "They can, and they will." To see the future, simply weigh together these predominant patterns:

1. Population development. During the following 20 years, the population of the United States will increase by 40 million people.

2. Incomes. During the following 20 years, representatives, business visionaries, experts, and entrepreneurs will see their incomes ascend by more than 50 percent.

3. Country estates. During the following 20 years, in any event, 10 million additional Americans (and remote nationals) will buy country estates inside the United States.

4. Echo boomers. During the following 20 years, above 60 million reverberation boomers (kids and grandkids of the people born after WW2) will enter the lodging business sector to buy homes.

5. Confinements on advancement. During the following 20 years, zoning, natural laws, building guidelines, and land deficiencies will continue to limit advancement in those regions where a great many people need to live.

6. Development costs. During the following 20 years, the expenses to develop houses (and different sorts of structures) will pursue their past pattern line upward.

7. Foreigners and minorities. Right now, just 40 percent of our quickest developing foreigner and minority gatherings (Hispanics, blacks, Asians) claim their own homes. Conversely, more than 75 percent of whites live in homes they possess. With government projects and loan specialist outreach endeavors going all out, during the following 20 years, people in these minority and worker gatherings will continue to buy homes in record numbers. Administrative, state, and neighborhood governments in participation with private banks will endeavor to close the home possession hole.

8. Financial specialists. During the following 20 years, over 60 million children of post-war, America will require a retirement salary. They will progressively go to venture land to address this issue. Interest for a property as speculation will continue to detonate—as it has during the previous 5 years.

You don't need propelled information about financial matters and socioeconomics to perceive the way that each significant social pattern is pushing land costs upward. Every year and consistently, the Federal Reserve framework increase the cash supply. As more cash pursues a gradually expanding inventory of properties, property costs go up—even without a general great change in the basic powers of the organic market (advertise appreciation). The Federal Reserve explicitly structures its financial strategies to make a humble (1.5 to 3.0 percent) yearly addition in the Consumer Price Index (CPI). Occasionally, however, the Fed loses control of inflationary cost increases (the late 1940s, the whole 1970s, ahead of schedule to mid-1980s). During those superheated, inflationary occasions, land costs will regularly encounter inflationary additions of 6 to 12 percent a year.

Interest rate and Inflation

Journalists over and over sustain the fantasy that our purported "current generally low home loan financing costs" have caused the ongoing value run-ups in lodging. In actuality, the present 30-year home loan financing costs of 5 to 7 percent just appear to be low comparative with those home loan paces of 8 to 16 percent that we encountered all through a significant part of the 1970s and 1980s. During the greater part of our nation's 225 or more years of history, contract loan costs ordinarily have extended somewhere in the range of 3 and 6 percent. Along these lines, the present rates remain toward the high-normal finish of history— not the historically low. Be that as it may, in any case, you may ask, what befalls real estate prices if interest rates do go up?

Higher Interest Rates Are Caused by Higher Inflation

Long haul interest rates climbed significantly during the 1970s and 1980s because the Consumer Price Index (inflation) bounced from the to some degree gentle yearly degrees of 2.5 to 4.0 percent of the ahead of schedule to mid-1960s as far as possible up to 13 percent in 1982. Also, for the record, you may take note of that during those 16 years of expanding inflation and soaring interest rates (from the 1970s 6.0 percent to 1981's 16 percent), most property values about significantly increased. Albeit higher inflation drives up interest rates, inflation likewise drives up rent levels and development costs. Surprisingly better for speculators who claim the real estate, when inflation warms up, the keen cash escapes budgetary resources (stocks and bonds) for hard resources (real estate, gold, collectibles). Subsequently, property prices are pushed much higher as stock and bond prices stagnate or decay. For instance, in 1964, the securities exchange's Dow Jones Industrial Average crested at near 1,000. In 1981, it sat at under 800—20 percent underneath its high characteristic of 17 years sooner. During this equivalent 17-year time of higher interest rates and inflation across the country, middle house prices zoomed from $25,000 to almost $75,000. History demonstrates that over long periods, higher interest rates don't hurt property values. An incredible opposite, higher interest rates (which just reflect high inflation) impel property prices to new record statures.

Higher Interest Rates? Lower Interest Rates? You Gain Either Way

Let's assume you purchase today and secure a long-haul home loan interest rate of 6.5 percent. On the off chance that interest rates go down, you can renegotiate and exploit lower installments. However, if inflation again goes wild and interest rates head up to 8, 10, 12 percent or higher, you'll gain as inflation drives the price of your property up and cuts the real dollar (inflation-balanced) measure of your home loan balance. You obtain dollars when their buying force is solid. You pay them back when their purchasing force has fallen. You gain. Your bank loses.

Dissimilar to contract loan specialists in numerous nations, banks in the United States must convey the unfriendly dangers made by both higher interest rates and lower interest rates. At the point when rates go down, you can renegotiate. At the point when rates go up because of inflation, you can gather higher rents and pay your advance off in modest dollars. Despite which heading interest rates move, real estate financial specialists (contract borrowers) procure the increases for themselves.

Cash Flows

Many real estate's produce cash flows from rent accumulations. Even though the present cash flows (in some extravagant pieces of the nation) currently lose unleveraged returns of only 4 to 8 percent a year, those cash flows make certain to increment after some time. At the point when mixed, inflation and market demand can push rents up a normal of 3 to 5 percent a year. Inside 15 years, the present rent level of $1,000 a month can increment to $1,500 to $1,800 every month (or conceivably more). You likewise will have the option to support your cash flows during periods when interest rates decrease. State that, because of a renegotiate at a lower interest rate, the home loan installment on your speculation property tumbles from $2,000 every month to $1,700 every month. That renegotiate simply put another $300 every long stretch of cash stream into your pocket.

Envision for a minute that inflation closures and market demand (property gratefulness) slow down. You gather just enough rents from your property to pay your working costs and home loan installments. With dormant rent accumulations and property values, have you made a poor venture? Not under any condition. As mortgage balance is being paid off by you, your equity in the property continues to grow—even without an increase in your property's value.

Purchase Below Market Value

In real estate, you can profit the minute you purchase a property. In contrast to most different ventures, you can purchase real estate for not as much as its market value. Bothered proprietors, proprietors who need to sell quickly and bother free, loan specialists who possess abandonment (called REOs), and inadequately educated vendors now and again part with their properties at prices (or terms) that promptly placed dollars into your total assets. A few investors flip properties they purchase at a bargain price to produce fast money. Others hold if possible and utilize the bargain price (or terms) to help their long-term benefits. In any case, bargain prices fill your financial balances with cash.

Create Value with Property Improvements

Most investors (and mortgage holders) neglect to deliberately improve their properties to augment values. Therefore, enterprising investors—an investor like you who can spot open doors for improvements—can significantly and rapidly support the values of the properties you purchase. Furthermore, when you work smartly, you additionally gain because your properties get higher rents.

Different Ways to Improve

At the point when we talk about property improvement, most proprietors search just revenue-driven rolling out restorative improvements: Lay some new rug, paint the dividers, tidy up the yard, and put new tile floors in the kitchen and restrooms. You can (and should) go a long way past beautifier. As an imaginative enterprising investor, you will build up an all-out fix-up and redesign plan that may include kitchen and shower rebuilding, re-configuring a story plan, including lookout windows or roof stature, and upper room or cellar transformations. As an enterprising investor, you will review contending properties, search for unsatisfied inhabitant (purchaser) needs, and after that, deliberately structure an arrangement of improvement to create the wow factor. With wow factors set up, you won't just add to the value of your structure; you will draw in topflight occupants and gather higher rents.

Improve the Neighbors and Neighborhood

"Purchase in the best neighborhood you can manage. The best neighborhoods consistently value the quickest." So, says one of the most seasoned buzzwords in real estate. In any case, truth be told, it's the turnaround neighborhoods that can frequently shoot up in value the most. All through the United States, numerous once oppressed and disregarded neighborhoods have encountered improvement. Albeit a few investors trust that these neighborhoods will give solid indications of restoration, different investors hop in ahead of schedule while prices are still absolute bottom modest. They discover neighborhoods that show potential. At that point, they work with other property proprietors, neighborhood inhabitants, nearby government, and not- for-benefits to create network rejuvenation.

In any case, you can benefit hugely. In any event, during those periods when normal property prices and rent levels simply edge up (level off or turn down), a few neighborhoods stay prime contenders for fast price heightening. Turnaround neighborhoods allow you to realize each investor's fantasy, "Purchase low, sell high."

Convert the Use

Occasionally, some real estate market gets overbuilt with lofts, places of business, strip malls, service stations, or different kinds of property. At the point when such overbuilding happens, ready investors go bargain chasing. Albeit some bargain trackers hold if possible, others go for the snappy benefits by changing over properties starting with one utilize then onto the next. For instance, New York City currently experiences an excess of office space and reducing the place of business rents. Interestingly, apartment rentals and housing prices keep on ascending considering New York's unending deficiency of homes and condos. Things being what they are, what course to benefits are some New York real estate investors taking? You got it. They're purchasing places of business for next to nothing and changing over this abundance office space into lofts and apartment suites.

Shield Your Profits from the IRS (Tax Shelter)

To build riches, you should shield your profit from the ravenous hand of government. Luckily, the income tax laws license proprietors of property to escape taxation in at any rate four significant ways:

- • Serial home selling
- • Section 1031 exchanges
- • Depreciation
- • Retirement planning

Serial Home Sellers

Developing quantities of Americans are profiting from putting resources into their homes tax-free. Here are how it works. By and large, when you claim a venture property, you will pay a capital increases tax on your resale profits at the time you sell. Be that as it may, when you sell your habitation, your additions come to you tax-free up to $250,000 ($500,000 for couples). For whatever length of time that you have lived in the property for two of the past five years, you need not report this profit to the IRS. Stunningly better, you can rehash this buy and deal at regular intervals. In a perfect world, you locate a home with solid fix-up and remodel potential.

Get it. Make esteem. Resell and reinvest your tax-free profits in extra properties. Proceed with this procedure until you accomplish your ideal degree of riches (or until you feel worn out on moving). For singles or couples without youngsters, serial home proprietorship can demonstrate to be an exceptional technique for producing moderately fast, tax-free profits. Or then again, if that you do have children, get them included. Set them to work. They'll become familiar with some significant exercises about land revamping and contributing.

Section 1031 Exchanges

Notwithstanding purchasing and selling a progression of individual habitations tax-free, you can likewise sell your speculation properties tax-free. You should simply adhere to the guidelines as set out in Section 1031 of the Internal Revenue Code. Pro realty professionals can without much of a stretch set up the essential administrative work to draw off these tax-free "exchanges." I put the exchange in citations since it's extremely a misnomer. You don't need to exchange your property with another proprietor. You sell one property and purchase another inside a time of a while.

Depreciation

In many organizations, the IRS taxes your net cash yearly income. Be that as it may, when you claim investment properties, you can shield (secure) a lot of your cash stream from taxes by utilizing a non-cash tax reasoning called depreciation. State your loft building (select of land esteem) is worth $500,000. Your pretax cash income from that property rises to $20,000 every year. In any case, you don't pay taxes on that $20,000 of income. You just pay taxes on $1,950 ($20,000 of income less $18,150 for passable depreciation).

What befalls that $18,150 derivation for depreciation if, state, your investment property yields just $10,000 per year in pretax cash income? In that circumstance, you might have the option to discount (deduct) that $8,150 ($18,150 deterioration less $10,000 property salary) of unused "misfortune" from the taxable sums you acquire from your other taxable pay (compensation, business benefits, intrigue, profits).

Tax-Deferred Retirement Plans

Do you claim an IRA retirement plan? Provided that this is true, you might have the option to invest all or part of it in real estate. Shockingly, the vast majority accept that they can just invest these retirement funds in corporate America's stocks, bonds, common funds, or currency market accounts. Wrong! Patrick Rice completely clarifies these real estate investing procedures in his book, IRA Wealth: Revolutionary IRA Strategies for Real Estate Investment (Garden City Park, N.Y., Square One, 2003, p. 3). This is what Rice says:

After the sharp decrease of the securities exchange, a considerable lot of us could just hold on and watch as our retirement reserve funds lost their amassed worth. Maybe a couple [investors] realized that there was an alternative that offered both wellbeing and development. That alternative is real estate. In opposition to what you may have accepted, it is conceivable and flawlessly legitimate to hold real estate in an IRA account—and to appreciate remarkable returns.

If you have developed funds in a tax-favored retirement fund, I ask you to converse with a money related genius or read Rice's book. Very likely, you will think that it's savvy to enhance in any event a segment of your IRA monies into real estate. IRA funds invested in real estate develop tax-free inside that record only equivalent to would stocks, bonds, and CDs.

How to Determine a Good Property

Savvy financial specialists comprehend that to be fruitful in the investment property business, they bring to the table the correct type of asset in the correct location and at the correct cost. Provided that you are simply beginning in the land business, you are probably going to have loads of questions. One of the principal questions that normally rings a bell is, "The thing that type of house should I purchase?" There are such a significant number of decisions accessible that just because speculator, it can appear to be overpowering. If you feel overpowered, don't surrender! What you are feeling is flawlessly ordinary. There are numerous choices to make, and as a future proprietor of investment properties, perhaps the greatest choice to make will be the type of house to buy. Your choice procedure will incorporate a few significant variables. You should think about the house's location, the type of neighborhood it is in, and the type of house it is.

You likewise should think about the age of the property and its physical condition. Likewise, you should consider the price tag and terms. The cost and terms of the house are high for two reasons. The principal reason is that your occupants must have the option to manage the cost of it, and the subsequent reason is that it must have a cash flow that bodes well as a venture for you. Before you can decide whether the rental unit will give enough cash flow, you'll have to realize how a lot of leases to charge. When you have limited the determination to a few competitors, you can break down the salary and expenses and measure their profits against the investment criteria you have set for yourself.

One noteworthy factor to remember all through the determination procedure is to be patient. It is alright to be anxious, energized, and prepared to begin when you purchase your first investment property. This is incredible. Simply recall that your essential purpose behind getting into this business is to profit, so be smart and take as much time as is needed before bouncing into anything. Smart financial specialists are patient, and patient speculators are also smart.

How to Choose the Right Location

As a brilliant financial specialist who is in the investment property business, you need to be cautious about where your units are found. The kind of location most appropriate for investment properties is regularly in a local that is somewhere in the range of 10 and 35 years old. These neighborhoods speak to areas where the normal middle-class native lives. Neighborhoods more youthful than 10 years old will, in general, have bigger and progressively costly homes, while neighborhoods older than 35 years old are frequently kept running down and in declining areas of town. This isn't generally the situation since they're a few areas at least 40 years old that keep on being all around kept up and where pride of proprietorship exists. The 35-year age standard is where the inclination for homes and neighborhoods older than that is probably going to decrease in worth.

One cogent factor to consider when picking a location is your holding period. At the end of the day, to what extent do you intend to keep the house? If you are going to keep a rental unit until the home loan is satisfied, state, 25, or 30 years, and the house you are thinking about is as of now nearing the finish of its monetary life expectancy, you might need to rethink. Obtaining an investment property that you intend to hold for 30 years that is as of now 30 years old may not be to your greatest advantage. Basic expansion discloses to us that the house will be 60 years old when you prepare to sell it, and by at that point, it likely could be considered practically out of date, which is a considerate method for saying that it is good for nothing to anybody. Then again, on the event that you intend to keep the house for just 5 to 10 years, your choice to buy an older house is most likely alright. The perfect location for speculators is one in which most of the houses are very much kept and in an area that isn't declining. The area ought to be settled, have great schools close by, and be in a tolerably solid exchange showcase. Networks of this sort regularly show such qualities as develop finishing, extravagant yards, and homes that are in generally great condition.

Selecting the Right Type of House

There are just about the same number of various kinds of houses as there are individuals, or so it appears. For instance, there are one-bedroom productivity units, there are marginally bigger two-bedroom houses, and there are three-and four-bedroom houses also. A few houses may have carports, though others may have secured parking spaces. A few houses may have a porch, while others may have a deck. A few houses might be a one-story farm, while others might be two-story colonials. With such huge numbers of decisions, it's occasionally hard to figure out which type is the most appropriate for your venture purposes.

The smart financial specialist will assess the encompassing business sector that is well on the way to influence her selection. Especially, you have to ask yourself, "Who will be my tenants, and where will they originate from?" For instance, if you live in a school town or almost a college, your tenants are probably going to be youthful understudies who are on a shoestring spending plan. This recommends you should focus your endeavors on discovering lodging that will best address their issues. As far as known generally, since the normal undergrad is working on a limited spending plan, she is ordinarily ready to forfeit every one of the additional items for a modest spot. This limits your selection to reasonable lodging units, for example, one-bedroom efficiencies or little two-bedroom houses with not very many frills. Undergrads don't require an enormous spot, they don't require a deck, they don't require a carport, and they don't need secured stopping. What they do need is modest lodging. For this specific market, you may considerably think about a little duplex or triplex structure.

Assume that you don't live in a school town or near a college. At that point what? Once more, analyze the market encompassing your region and figure out who your clients, or tenants, are well on the way to be. The biggest pool of forthcoming tenants in many regions comprises of families with somewhere in the range of one to upwards of four youngsters, with the normal being around two. These families generally require a few bedroom houses with a couple of showers and a couple of vehicle carport. Keep in mind that, when in doubt, individuals who lease can't bear to purchase for some reason. It might be that they don't procure enough or maybe have an inadequate record as a consumer. Whatever the reason might be isn't as significant as to perceive that most families are on a constrained spending plan. Thus, they commonly look for fundamental living lodging.

This implies in your pursuit to choose the correct kind of lodging. You need to remember these realities. You regularly should search for unobtrusively measured houses with a few bedrooms that are reasonably evaluated comparatively with the market. The rents created from these properties must be adequate to cover every one of the costs, administration the obligation, and still have something left finished. The bit that is "left finished" speaks to your arrival on speculation (ROI), and that is the reason you're in the land business.

Physical Condition: Inspecting Is Key

A rental house's physical condition can run anyplace from amazingly poor, as in censured, to generally excellent, as in flawless. The type of property to concentrate on will depend fundamentally on your speculation goals. A few investors prefer to buy rental properties that are all around looked after, clean, and ready to go. Then again, a few investors prefer to buy rental properties that are needing some repair, regularly alluded to as fixer-uppers. The explanation that a few people prefer fixer-uppers is that they can buy them for less cash than a house that is ready to go. These people frequently contribute their time and work to include or make an incentive in the property, or they may even contract a jack of all trades to finish these assignments.

If it's all the same to you're the type of individual, who got on some additional work, at that point, your consideration should focus on houses that are needing just minor repairs. Buying rental houses that fall into this class will demonstrate to be the most productive because you will have the option to limit the measure of cash required for the necessary enhancements, consequently enabling you to amplify your ROI. Another worry is the time engaged with making significant repairs. The time required for rental houses that require just minor repairs is a lot shorter than it is for the individuals who require significant repairs. Provided that you are anticipating leasing the house out, at that point, the additional time you spend taking a shot at it, the more it will cost you in lost rents. Preferably, you need to start gathering rent when your first installment is expected. If you do choose to take on a fixer upper, I suggest that you search for a house that looks a great deal more awful than it truly is. Finally, you should search for a house that needs corrective type repairs, for example, new paint, arranging, and perhaps a decent cleaning. Cosmetic repairs are snappy and simple to make and are regularly the most affordable type of repair.

The accompanying investigation items give a review of things to search for in your evaluation of a house's physical condition.

Houses with frail or awful foundations ought to be maintained a strategic distance from completely because fixing foundations can be both tedious and costly. For instance, if the house is built on a solid chunk and significant settling has happened, the house should be leveled. Leveling a house not exclusively can be exorbitant. However, it additionally can be tedious. This will cost you cash in repairs just as lost rents. Moreover, houses with foundation problems are probably going to have other auxiliary harm brought about by the settling. A nearby investigation of the inside walls quite often will show proof of settling because the drywall will be broken and isolated. It is normal in numerous houses to see hairline cracks in walls, particularly around the creases, so don't be frightened if you see small cracks, for example, these. Detachment cracks can be fixed rapidly and effectively with a little filler, for example, caulk and a new layer of paint. On the off chance that, then again, you see enormous cracks running down the divider, you can nearly wager that the house has a foundation issue. You likewise ought to review the outside of the house. Specifically, if the house has some block on it, search for bigger than ordinary divisions in the mortar. Once more, don't stress over hairline cracks. These are ordinary. On the off chance that the house doesn't have a block, indications of a poor foundation can be seen around doorjambs and window outlines that are askew.

On the off event that the house was not built on a section yet was built with a cellar foundation; rather, you should be particularly mindful of dampness problems. This is genuinely normal, particularly in more seasoned homes. Search for cracks in the storm cellar walls that may have proof of spilling around them, for example, recoloring or buildup. Breaks in the walls additionally can make the development of form in the storm cellar territory, an issue that is turning into a significant risk for some property proprietors. It isn't at all bizarre to see small cracks in a storm cellar floor or even in the walls. You shouldn't be unnecessarily worried about these sorts of cracks since they are typically simply surface cracks that don't go completely through the floor or the divider. Similarly, as houses built on sections with foundation problems can be over the top expensive to fix, so can houses built on storm cellars with comparative problems. Your most safe and reasonable option is to stay away from storm cellar and section foundation problems. There is a plethora of houses that are in better condition which you can decide buying eventually.

Furthermore, significant repairs that are required can be signified by roofs to another zone. The cost to fix a roof can fluctuate broadly with age and condition. Most creation shingles have a base existence of 20 to 25 years, so if the current shingles are under 15 years old, it is an entirely sure thing that any fixes required would be insignificant. Following 15 years, the shingles can start twisting up and wearing to the point where holes may start to grow, so make certain to search for indications of this. One approach to decide whether the roof has been leaking is to take a gander at the roofs inside the house. If you watch water spots or stains, this is a generally excellent sign that the roof has been and might spill. Stains or wet spots in the attic are additionally a decent marker or sign.

Although older roofs regularly give indications of staining, it isn't phenomenal for more up to date roofs to progress toward becoming stained also. Stained roofs can be cleaned effectively and modestly by applying a substance procedure. The staining commonly is brought about by a development of buildup that can be executed and evacuated with an answer of water, blanch, and different synthetic substances that is accessible at most home improvement shops. On the off chance that another roof is required, the cost to supplant it may not be restrictive. If, for instance, another layer of shingles can be applied over the current layer, the cost and time included are insignificant. Then again, on the off chance that a few layers of shingles as of now exist, at that point, a tear-off likely will be vital. This can increase the cost of another roof essentially because the work required for the tear-off can be costly because of the additional time included. Moreover, more seasoned homes that, as of now, have a few layers of shingles on them may require still more work. The roof deck, which is more up to date homes is made of sheathing or pressed wood, might be harmed because of water releases that have happened after some time. On the off chance that the house should be totally re-decked, this will surely increase the fixed cost because of the extra time and materials required for substitution.

Different repairs that may appear to be exorbitant incorporate replacing equipment, windows, and outside surfaces, for example, block or siding. On the off chance that the heater and air conditioner are worn out, replacing them can rapidly add up. Expenses can go somewhere in the range of $1500 to $7500 contingent upon what should be done and the kind of hardware you replace. Replacing every one of the windows additionally can be expensive and can add thousands to the value you pay. Block and siding repairs, contingent upon the degree of wear or harm are another thing that can add up quickly. On the off chance that lone a couple of minor repairs are required, for example, replacing a couple of windows or screen entryways or applying new paint, at that point you are presumably really safe with your choice to buy the investment property, gave, obviously, that the remainder of your venture criteria are met.

The house's plumbing additionally ought to be checked cautiously for appropriate activity. The plumbing can be investigated effectively by flushing toilets, checking underneath sinks, and searching for leaky faucets. Make certain to check the age and state of the home's hot water warmer too. Leaky drain and hot water heaters are easy to repair and additionally replace and should be possible rapidly and reasonably. Progressively costly repairs that can add up rapidly include underground sewer lines, particularly on the off chance that they are implanted in a concrete section. These lines now and then can get broken on account of establishment issues, for example, settling. The division in the line doesn't enable the sewage to deplete appropriately, and furthermore, can make the line back up. Brilliant investors will limit managing the more serious kinds of plumbing issues, for example, damaged underground lines. While leaky water plumbing and hot water heaters are easy to repair or replace, broken or harmed sewer lines can be more enthusiastically to distinguish and cost considerably more to repair. A cautious review of the plumbing framework conceivably can spare you many dollars.

As a component of your inspection procedure, the home's electrical wiring additionally ought to be checked to guarantee that it is working properly. A basic check of outlets and light switches all through the house can disclose to you a lot about its electrical condition. If they are working properly, the odds are that the framework is alright. Houses that are 30 to 40 years of age or more may be checked more completely because they will, in general, have more issues. For instance, breakers and switches inevitably wear out and need substitution. In certain houses, the wiring might be old to the point that it should be supplanted totally. Supplanting the wiring in a house can be expensive because it is kept running behind the walls. An electrician likely should make slices in the drywall to expel and supplant the wiring. This implies when the electrician is done, the drywall should be fixed, and from that point onward, the walls should be repainted. Do you perceive how rapidly something like flawed wiring can include? Except if you happen to be an electrician, maintain a strategic distance from houses that have wiring issues.

I suggest that you contract an expert house inspection company. These companies play out an exceptionally thorough inspection and quite often discover things wrong. Remember this is the thing that they are getting paid to do. At the point when they complete their inspection, you can hope to get a far-reaching composed report. The report archives everything the investigator finds and regularly contains genuinely minor things. Except if you are set up for this, you might be frightened at all the things composed of the report. Inspection organizations report all that they discover since that is the thing that they are being paid to do, and they additionally do as such to secure themselves. In the case of something isn't reported, the purchaser may return to them in the wake of claiming the house and guarantee that the organization disregarded the inadequacy and thus sued for harms.

Inspection benefits often cost somewhere in the range of $150 up to $500, contingent upon the territory of the country in which you live and the size of the house.

How to Secure a Great Deal on Real Estate

Places to get Rental Houses

Setting aside the effort to locate the correct investment property for your real estate portfolio is imperative to your prosperity. Notwithstanding where you may live, there is constantly a wealth of speculation openings accessible, many which can be discovered right in your terrace. By utilizing an efficient and widely inclusive methodology, you will have the option to locate more investment properties than you have time or cash to put resources into. You should, in any case, to practice tolerance as you continued looking for the correct property. This is particularly valid for starting financial specialists since they are frequently energized and on edge to begin. While eagerness is unquestionably significant, it can push you into difficulty if you are not cautious. To be effective, you should have the option to stay fair-minded and objective in your examination. Oversee your investment activities with wisdom, take as much time as is needed, be intensive, and, a large portion of all, be quiet.

Here are eight unique techniques you can start utilizing right presently to locate incredible investment properties. You can use as few as 1 or 1 of the proposed techniques or the same number of as every one of the 8. It is suggested that you explore different avenues regarding a few of the strategies with which you are generally commonplace.

- 1. Classified advertisements
- 2. Real estate magazines

- 3. Internet searches
- 4. Billboards and signs
- 5. Real estate agents
- 6. Scouts
- 7. Professional affiliations
- 8. For sale by homeowners (FSBOs)

Classified Advertisements

Most nearby newspapers convey an area in the characterized publicizing for single-family houses that are accessible available to be purchased. Many these ads are set by realtors and are intended to invite you to call their workplaces. Search for ads that utilization such keywords as a speculation opportunity, incredible rental property, or starter home. This kind of elucidating language is generally characteristic of more established houses in built-up neighborhoods, which are what you are searching for. This type of ordered commercial merits setting aside the effort to approach. Regardless of whether for reasons unknown, the house is never again accessible or doesn't meet your venture goals, despite everything it gives you a chance to make an exchange with a sales specialist who may have the option to locate the correct kind of rental house that would better meet your requirements. On the off chance that the operator's posting doesn't end up being what you are searching for, she may allude you to somebody in her office who works in venture type properties.

A considerable lot of the ads recorded in the grouped segment are for sale by owners (FSBOs). Indeed, you need to search for keywords that may show the proprietor is restless to sell, can offer adaptable terms, or has a house that might be offered at a cost underneath retail. As you become progressively acquainted with costs in your nearby market, you will expand your capacity to perceive a decent arrangement when you see one. Numerous proprietors haven't the foggiest what their houses are extremely worth. In the event that, for instance, a proprietor has lived in a similar house for 20 or 30 years, he may not understand that home costs have expanded to the degree that they have and may in all likelihood be offering the house at a well beneath market cost. Some of you may feel this is exploiting such people.

At long last, you can utilize the classifieds to put your promotion in the land needed area. You don't have to spend a lot of cash on these ads. An elegantly composed and succinct promotion can be similarly as powerful as a bigger and progressively costly advertisement. You will likely get people who are inspired and need to sell their houses to call you. Your promotion ought to be intended to request the particular type of requiring the kind of rental house you are searching for with the goal that you are not troubled by people who are not prone to have the type of house available to be purchased for which you are looking. If you are searching for a specific type of house, for instance, a three-room, two-shower farm, in a specific value go, and with any exceptional terms, at that point be explicit and state that in your arranged promotion.

Real Estate Magazines

Practically all regions distribute books or magazines intermittently that are explicitly intended for private real estate deals. Often, you can find a few unique magazines, some for one territory and some for another. Real estate magazines can be found in numerous spots, including racks or newspaper kiosks situated outside real estate workplaces, medicate stores, and supermarkets. Real estate magazines can be an extraordinary hotspot for finding single-family houses. You likewise will find numerous real estate–related promoters that can be useful in these productions, for example, real estate agents, contract organizations, evaluation administrations, reviewing organizations, title organizations, real estate legitimate administrations, and insurance agencies. Most ads in these magazines are put by real estate agents; frequently, they will promote every one of their listings on one page. The ads generally include a photograph of the agent, alongside some convincing motivation behind why you should contact that agent for your real estate needs. Albeit most of the ads in real estate magazines are put by agents and expedites, a few magazines do offer an FSBO area. While a large portion of the business agents with listings in these productions center around the customary retail lodging section, there are frequently a few agents or firms that represent considerable authority in various specialties inside the real estate showcase.

Internet Searches

Various Web sites offer a wide range of information about houses available to be purchased. You can search in your general vicinity, or some other zone, just by entering in an expression, for example, "Homes available to be purchased Goodrich, MI," for instance. Such a search, for the most part, will produce aftereffects of 20 to 30 or considerably more Web sites with listings in your general vicinity. Most likely, the best-known site among all real estate sites highlighting houses available to be purchased is facilitated by the National Association of Realtors. You can discover this website on the Web at www.realtor.com. This site has more than 2 million listings for different sorts of properties, including single-family homes, condos, townhouses, multifamily lofts, manufactured homes, empty land, homesteads, and rentals. The information determined for these listings originate from the Multiple Listing Service, so it would exclude any FSBO properties. The site is accessible to the overall population, so you don't need to be a real estate operator to get to the listings on it. It is especially like an open numerous posting administration for properties made accessible to the overall public or anybody with a PC and access to the Web. You likewise can search by property type, state, city, postal division, value range, least and most extreme square feet, time of home, number of floors, and a few other criteria. Most listings give an elucidating diagram of the property, photographs, and contact information.

Other great Internet sources incorporate your nearby papers. Practically all significant papers currently list their whole grouped segment on Web sites. The information is frequently updated daily. This is normally dictated by how frequently the paper is distributed. For instance, if it is a daily paper, it is doubtlessly updated daily. A week after week paper would be updated week by week. A bit of leeway the paper Web sites offer over a webpage, for example, Realtor.com is that notwithstanding giving advertisements set by real estate agents, there are additionally numerous promotions put by people, for example, FSBO homes. Paper grouped promotions found on the Web are not so finish as those on a website, for example, Realtor.com, yet they do give you a decent blend of properties available to be purchased by both real estate agents and individual mortgage holders.

Billboards and Signs

As your organization develops and you have progressively accessible in your publicizing spending plan, you might need to consider utilizing billboards to promote that you buy houses. These signs can be viable, particularly in neighborhoods where the traffic tally is known to be high. One essential advantage of utilizing board promoting is the recurrence with which your message is seen. People who take a similar course to work for quite a while will pass by your sign.

They may not be keen on selling now, however sooner or later, they might just be, and regardless of whether they don't call you, they may tell a companion, relative, or associate about you. Another advantage of utilizing billboards is that, in all honesty, they are very cost-effective when contrasted and different types of promoting, for example, show advertisements in papers. For instance, if the normal day by day traffic check is 50,000 at a specific area, this is what could be compared to 1½ million people every month who will see your sign. The lower cost per thousand methods arriving at more people for less cash. One beneficial thing to remember when utilizing billboards is to keep your message basic by not putting an excessive amount of data on the sign. Drivers, as a rule, have only a concise minute to peruse your message as they pass by, so keep it basic and immediate, for example, "I buy houses! Call (949) 3333-7777." You may likewise consider utilizing smaller signs that are more affordable than huge, full-sized billboards. Smaller signs, for example, those estimating roughly 18 by 24 inches, typically are made from layered plastic and are genuinely economical to buy. You can buy them with wire casing stands that make them simple to put in high-traffic areas.

Scouts

Another extraordinary method to find potential investment openings is by utilizing a scout. A scout does precisely what the name recommends— the scouts for investment properties that meet your venture criteria. Scouts who served in the U.S. Armed force years back gave precious support of their commanders. They were conveyed ahead of time of the troops to accumulate data about the enemy's position, its military quality, and potential zones of helplessness. The scouts would then report back to their chief to give key data about the enemy. Significant choices were then made dependent on the data assembled by the scouts. While military authorities depended intensely on scouts 200 years prior, they currently utilize a significantly more propelled kind of scout. The present military pioneers depend on complex innovation, for example, radar and satellite symbolism to report fundamental data, for example, the enemy's position, what number of tanks the enemy has on the ground, and what number of troops the enemy has set up. The procedure itself is a lot of the equivalent, however, with significant data being given to those approved to decide. Similarly, as the scouts in the military report indispensable knowledge to the individuals who could follow up on it, so do scouts in a land limit report key data concerning potential speculation chances to you. A decent scout should accumulate; however, much data as could be expected with the goal that you can settle on reasonable choices.

Scouts such material information as:

- • The general state of the investment property
- • The property area
- • A local evaluation

- • The merchant's asking value, terms, and timing needs
- • The vender's explanation behind selling and the level of criticalness
- • Comparable deals information identified with the zone

On the off chance that utilizing scouts is new to you, you might consider how to approach discovering one who can bring opportunities to you. Essentially anybody can fill in as a scout on the grounds that there are no licenses to get. For example, there are realtors. Besides, no specific preparing is required other than the directions you give them concerning the kinds of investment properties you are searching at, the value range, and data, for example, that recorded previously. For instance, you can offer to pay a referral charge of $500 to undergrads, companions, neighbors, or relatives for each arrangement they present to you that outcomes in a purchase.

Professional Affiliations

Your association with or participation in a professional association is another extraordinary method to discover investment properties. Proficient associations incorporate neighborhood gatherings, for example, the council of trade and national gatherings, for example, the National Association of Home Builders. Numerous regions likewise have land venture related affiliations and clubs. Your participation in an expert association gives you an astounding chance to connect with other people who offer comparative interests. Individuals frequently incorporate financial specialists such as yourself, land agents, assessment and land lawyers, surveyors, appraisers, and horde different experts. Proficient associations commonly have occasional gatherings in which data is shared that might be of an incentive to you? Numerous gatherings meet month to month, for instance, at a nearby café for breakfast. Visitor speakers, much of the time, are included at the gatherings and give their aptitude as it identifies with a given theme. You can discover real estate associations in your general vicinity by looking in the Yellow Pages or by doing an Internet search utilizing an expression, for example, "land venture clubs."

I urge you to join at any rate a couple of expert associations and to turn into a functioning member in them. You will likely meet individuals and to build up associations with them. You need to widen your range of prominence by becoming more acquainted with the same number of individuals as you can, particularly those with whom you share comparative interests. Make certain to tell others what it is you do as a land financial specialist and what sorts of houses you are searching for. Even though connections set aside an effort to create, no one can tell when this sort of system administration will satisfy you. It might simply be that the individual you are conversing with happens to consider selling his home and couldn't want anything more than to work out an arrangement with you.

FSBOs

Individuals who like to sell their very own houses frequently are alluded to as FSBOs. Sellers who fall into this gathering commonly advertise their houses in a couple of ways. The primary thing they do is go to the local tool shop and purchase an "Available to be purchased By Owner" sign, a dark enchantment marker, and a stand. Next, they compose their phone number on the sign, and after that, gladly spot it in the front yard for all to see. Some FSBOs venture to such an extreme as to buy two signs and spot the subsequent one down the road at the crossing point. After the signs have been set, the seller frequently will call the local newspaper to run an ordered promotion for up to 14 days. Following 30 to 60 days with practically no achievement, most of FSBOs become baffled and in the long run, enroll the administrations of an expert, that is, an authorized realtor.

     Even though the FSBOs' motivation to set aside cash by abstaining from paying a land commission is justifiable, what they neglect to acknowledge is that there is considerably more to selling a house than simply putting a sign out in the front yard. Regardless of whether you're selling utilized vehicles or houses, selling is tied in with advertising and presentation. A sign in the front yard brings about notifying every one of the neighbors that the house is available to be purchased; however very little more. What number of neighbors will be keen on purchasing the house? Most likely relatively few. Signs are valuable, in any case, to help purchasers driving from another zone to even more effectively distinguish the house's area. Promoting in the local newspaper will support a few, yet in little to moderate-sized towns, the seller is yet constraining himself to the prompt network.

Purchasing Rental Property

There are numerous reasons why people progressed toward becoming landlords or engage with leasing and managing an investment property, and these reasons can be very basic. A few people get into investment property the executives knowing there is a lot of work yet seeking after great income and property appreciation (that is, the value increases during the time you possess the property). Others may get bulldozed, rather than owning an investment property. Some of the time, people move out of the zone either because of work or a choice to take a vacation for a year or two. They may choose not to sell their homes since they have plans to return. In these circumstances, the home was never intended to be an investment property, however getting pay on the property helps take care of the month to month tabs. In different cases, a parent gets more established and should move to a helped living office. The family wouldn't like to sell the home for specific reasons. Now, they investigate leasing the home to help pay the parent(s) month to month costs and along these lines hold the property for a legacy.

Ways of acquiring property

The following segments examine a portion of the manners in which you can transform your present home into an investment property.

Job transfer/temporary assignment

Executives and professionals are sometimes transferred temporarily from where they own home to another city or even another country for a specific amount of time. I know I've worked with many employees who expected to be overseas for about two years and wanted to rent their homes while they're out of the country. You need to weigh your specific circumstances to determine the best way to proceed. If you will be out of state or country, you need to investigate a professional property management company. I don't suggest that you depend on a close companion or family member to deal with your home while you are away, aside from as a neighborhood crisis contact, yet that ought to be its degree. Remember that anything that a companion or family member says or does is equivalent to if it originated from you. They may truly need to support you yet might not have the opportunity to stay aware of the laws and deal with the upkeep.

Rather, start with a consultation with a property chief or rental agent. Discover what the rental worth is and what ought to be done to rent the property rapidly to a quality inhabitant. An ideal approach to rent your home is empty. Renting your property empty is a lot simpler in many markets than renting out your home with most of the furniture inside. Not exclusively are there more people searching for empty properties. However, people likewise will, in general, remain longer when they bring their possessions. If you choose to leave goods in the property, don't expect that they will be immaculate and impeccable when you return. Two or three years of mileage can be a great deal contingent upon the way of life of the renters. Now and again, a dish may get broken, and your example is never again accessible — presently, what?

I realize the issue is storage and what you can keep on the property. There are times that proprietors keep the basement, or back-yard storage shed to store things they won't require while they are no more. Lock this territory independently and give way into your property, the board organization. Remember that this territory must be illuminated in the rent as having a place with the proprietor and won't be a piece of the rented property. If you have numerous things that you will leave, investigate storage. There are storage organizations that will bring a canister to your carport, leave it for you to pack, and take it to their distribution center to store.

This spares your trips to a storage unit and might be paid for by your company as a major aspect of the movement cost. Commonly, when a worker is transferred by a business, a lot of the expenses and costs are dealt with by the company. The things you might need to request are property, the executives' charges, stockpiling charges, rental recompense in the event that you are called home preceding the finish of the rent with your inhabitant, and a portion of the costs required to rent your home. This may incorporate evolving locks, cleaning, additional protection, etc. Try not to leave anything of incredible incentive at the property while it is being rented.

Additionally, when are you being transferred, you should be certain that you deal with sending your mail and changing the utilities. It is a smart thought to make duplicates of the guidance manuals for machines, gear, and security frameworks to leave for the occupants. (In the event that you leave the real manuals behind, you may find that the manuals get pressed with the inhabitant's possessions when they leave.) Sometimes, when you are away for two years, you may think it is smarter to rent your property for two entire years.

As a proprietor renting your property, you can be very passionate about your home, so I exceptionally suggest you venture back and procure an expert. Remember that a portion of the valuable recollections you have aren't adequate to an inhabitant. If you have a development graph for your youngsters on the wall, for instance, you might need to snap a photo or follow it onto a bit of paper. I knew somebody who cut it out, fixed the wall, and put away this memory with their furnishings. This segment additionally applies on the off chance that you have lost your job locally and have needed to leave the territory to find a job. If you like your home, you just may settle on the choice to keep it for several years. You can't be sure whether the other job will be perpetual, or you might need to move back sometime in the future.

Moving to a nursing home

At the point when a parent gets older, the person may need to move to a helped living office or a rest home. There are alternatives, and one of them is to lease the home to help with the costs and maintain a strategic distance from expense liabilities. To comprehend these suggestions, you must look for the counsel of your expense proficient. Keeping the home likewise keeps the legacy unblemished and may give assets to crises that are not canvassed in some other way. On the off chance that the house has never been a rental, you may require some time to expel most of the possessions that have been gathered over numerous years.

Frequently, the home has not been refreshed or updated for quite a while and will require a considerable amount of work. Contract an expert to reveal to you what should be done to prepare the property and to give you a gauge of the rental incentive for cost arranging. Being readied is significant, as this is generally a passionate time for your mom and additionally father. On the off chance that they are capable, incorporate your folks in the plans. Have them there when you meet with the property the board organization and let them be a piece of the arranging and renting of their home. I see that you need as reasonable with the time it will take and know the bearing you must go to prepare the property. This helps a lot with the passionate side just as your long-term arrangements for renting the home.

Death of a parent

The death of a parent while living in the home is also an emotional time and one that requires you to take some time to decide what the next step will be. Planning and following similar steps to get the property ready as you would if they were moving to an assisted living home is the way to go, but in this case, allow more time. Take things slowly and easily if you can; taking a bit longer helps with the healing as well. Remember that if someone has died on the property, this must be disclosed to any potential renter.

The property you've tried to sell

If the property you are living in now isn't selling, and you have already committed to purchasing another property, you may consider renting out the property. Sometimes, the market turns around in a year or so, or you find that you enjoy having your first home as a rental. Be sure to meet with your accountant and/or your financial planner to be certain that renting your home is what is best for you currently.

Don't overcommit; stretch, but not too far. If you calculate that you'll lose money by continuing to try to sell, you may find you would be better off renting the property. The loss may be less than selling the property at a time when the market is down. Normally, the rental market goes along the sales market — but not most times. So, renting out your present home may make a lot of sense, especially if you are moving around November or December when market values are historically lower than the spring and summer. Sometimes it is also better to rent six months to a year in the area you are moving to. This allows you to make sure you are buying your new home in the right area.

Tips for Purchasing an Investment Property

When interest rates are low and the stock market unstable, buying an investment property may be a good choice for your financial portfolio. If so, there are items you will want to review before making that purchase. The mantra, "Location, location, location," applies to rental units just as it does to your own home.

Compare property values and rents

Do your homework first. Decide on the area in which you are thinking of purchasing. Speak to other friends, if possible, about their investments: where they own and how things are going. After you decide on an area or at least a county or city, look into the area's property values and juxtapose them against the property you are considering for purchase (before you make an offer and get into contract). You need to look at the property values and see comparable rentals in that area. If you see large swings or confusing figures, ask questions. If rents seem very low, find out why. You also want to check with the Chamber of Commerce or your city planning department to see whether any major changes are in store for the area the property is located in. Just imagine if you bought an investment property and found out a month later that a major freeway was going to go through one block away!

Investigate various loan options

Check all loans meticulously to have a feel of how they will perform in the future. Many adjustable-rate loans can change the property from a good investment to a bad one if the interest rates skyrocket. Many investors choose interest-only loans to maximize their return on investment. Be realistic — anything can happen.

Consider the property tax

Often, investors base their purchases on current property tax laws. Then the taxes increase when they buy at a higher property value. Don't get caught in this trap. Find out the state tax laws and possible tax changes, and incorporate the new, projected property tax into your figures.

Take into account supplemental tax

In some states, when purchasing a property, you are responsible for paying a supplemental tax. This is usually a local tax paid to your county tax assessor. In California, for example, you receive a supplemental tax bill to be paid in two payments. The amount due is a percentage of the previous owners' assessed value as compared to the price you paid currently for the property. For example, if the previous owner paid $200,000, and you paid $400,000 for the same property, the property is reassessed, and the new value is the price you paid: $400,000. Your nearby tax office sends you a supplemental tax bill due in two installments for a level of that $200,000 contrast. This bill is notwithstanding your ordinary property duty bill; however (fortunately), it doesn't exist in certain states.

Confirm utility costs

Investigate with the local sewer, water, and garbage companies to see whether the utility companies will bill the tenant. Often, on multiple units, you pay for the water and garbage. Ask for copies from the past year of the renter-paid utilities and the water and garbage. This will give you a general idea of what to expect for those expenses. Keep in mind that when the rental property has two units or more, you will be paying the common area utilities, which usually includes the outside lights, sprinklers, and laundry room. Some multiple units have a common water heater, and others have a separate water heater in each unit — so be sure you include this cost. Common area heating, air conditioning, and lighting will also be your responsibility. If there is a swimming pool or other facilities, the utility costs will be even higher.

Check on insurance coverage

Similarly, as the duty bill can increment, so can insurance. Moreover, you will need to fuse a "landlord/rental" policy into your assessments that will give you more protection than the standard property holder's protection arrangement. Try not to be frightened; most landlords' policies are a sensible expense, even though in numerous states that have seen late cataclysmic events, all insurance policies have expanded a lot. Find out whether there have been any claims in the last three years. Before closing the deal, be sure that you can get insurance on the property.

Plan for future maintenance costs

What property you purchase will figure out what you should spend on support.

If you have a chance to buy a fixer- upper, you must acquire reasonable evaluations.

Be careful with the snare of not getting ready for any support, basically because you have acquired a property in amazing condition. Think about your living arrangement and the time and vitality required to maintain that property. There is always something. If the property possesses a swimming pool, landscaping, or other facilities, monthly maintenance expenses will be included to pay. Check out home warranty companies. There are others that will cover your property, which will mitigate unexpected expenses and the inconvenience of finding contractors to take care of the maintenance problems.

Consult your accountant/financial planner and real estate agent

Tax laws can change, and your financial picture may change with them. Make sure that you talk to people who are knowledgeable about investment property. Remember, tax laws may change later, but if you choose the right property with the right financing, it will weather the changes.

Inspect the property

Always be sure to perform a thorough inspection of the property before buying. If you can't do this personally do, use someone reliable to do it for you. Hiring a professional inspector to examine the structural and mechanical systems of the property is also a sound investment. Get the facts before signing a long-term commitment and a long-term loan.

When conducting the inspections, you usually need both pest control and a contractor's inspection. There are a few items that are often overlooked that should also be inspected during your inspection time.

The roof

I would always have a professional roofing company inspect the roof to determine the condition and the estimated life remaining before it will need replacement. This is a large expense and one you should be prepared and budget for. A leaky roof is a major problem itself but also can lead to additional problems down the road. Water can do a great deal of damage to the structure of a building and require major repairs or replacement. The time of year when you purchase a property may make it difficult to look for leaks. Hire a professional to inspect the roof.

Chimneys

Often people forget to have the chimney of the fireplace checked. The buildup of creosote or cracks in the firebox is fire dangers. This can also be an unexpected expense.

Pool

If the property has a pool, have the pool, as well as any associated equipment, checked and inspected. You need to be certain everything is up to code, as a pool can be a large expense, and many local and state ordinances go with having a pool. If the pool is used in a multiple unit setting, be certain that all your proper signs are posted along with any required safety equipment.

Survey

Some people have a professional survey performed on a potential property. This way, you know your exact property lines and what is expected of you as the landlord within those boundaries.

Engineer's report

There are times that a prospective owner should get a soil engineer's report, especially with a property located on the side of a hill. This is quite common in California, as well as in other places. An engineer has access to reports that display flood plains, sinkholes, and other geological hazards. Having all these reports done is not only costly but also takes up a great deal of time. This is for your protection and the long-term maintenance of your investment. Take the time to do the inspections you need to feel comfortable about purchasing the property.

Methods of Structuring a Purchase

Lease/Option: A lease option gives you the right to purchase a property at a certain price and terms on or before a certain date. In the meantime, you take over the operation of the property on a lease basis. You are leaving the house or investment property from the seller. You are not obligated to a formal contract where you must close or lose your deposit. Generally, you must put up some option money to get a seller to take his property off the market while you decide to close on the transaction or to pass. If you decide not to buy, the seller keeps the option money. If you do close on the property, the option money becomes part of the down payment. Why would you want to option it rather than an outright contract to buy? First, it gives you the opportunity of handling rentals and taking care of renovations. It gives you control of the property without being obligated to the total ownership cost and obligation. Perhaps you need time to close on another property to afford this one, and you are not sure it will close. If it doesn't, you are not obligated to buy this one.

Tip:

If you have negotiated a good price and terms on a property, you may want to consider selling your option to another investor. You can run a blind ad offering a "below market" price on a home in an excellent neighborhood. Must sell! This type of ad will draw some response. Notice I suggested a "blind" ad. You don't want the seller to know you are shopping for his contract with you at a higher price.

Lease/Purchase:

A lease-purchase obligates you to close on the transaction within a certain time frame. It is not an option. It is a firm commitment to buy. Again, the purpose is to give you time to handle rentals and renovation, without taking over the full liability of ownership. One advantage to both alternatives is that you can tie up a property for a couple of months or longer at today's price. The seller may want a price adjustment if you wait for some time to close.

Individual Corporation:

This method requires you to set up a corporation with you as the President and probably the sole officer other than a spouse who will be Secretary/Treasurer. There may be a certain liability and tax benefits to a corporate structure.

Pros: For certain investors, there could be tax benefits in corporate ownership. It also can take away personal liability if the property is held corporately.

Cons: You are now dealing with a corporation that must follow a different set of guidelines than you would as a private owner. There is also a possibility of double taxation, both as a corporation and as an individual who takes money out of the corporation. Seek legal and/or tax counsel for details.

Partnerships:

This is a way of obtaining additional funding. You find a partner with some money who wants to enter into a joint venture partnership with you. He puts up the money, and you do the work and have the marketing expertise to structure a profitable investment for both of you.

Pros: It is a way of finding the cash to consummate the purchase

Cons: You now have a partner in the ownership of the property. Partners tend to disagree with it. If they do and decide to dissolve the partnership agreement, you have two choices:

1. Buy out the partner, which requires mutual agreement of the fair market value of his or her interest.

2. Sell the property and divide the proceeds.

Important Point: A partnership does not have to be a 50/50 arrangement. You can negotiate any equity share that you both agree on when preparing the partnership agreement. For example, you are doing all of the work locating and purchasing the property, renovation, and management of the asset and eventually selling it. The partner merely put in some cash, probably a small percentage of the overall investment in the property, which is probably the total cost of the property. The partner should not expect to be an equal partner in the transaction. There is a better way.

Limited Partnerships:

A limited partnership is exactly what the term implies. You take on one or more partners in the purchase of your property. These partners are limited partners because they have no say in the operation of the property. You would serve as the General Partner and be responsible for the entire operation of the investment. This means you will put the transaction together, negotiate the purchase, manage the property, and determine when it is to be sold.

Pros: This puts you in full charge of the operation, and you do not have to worry about a conflict with a partner. You are the controlling factor. The limited partner or partner's involvement is only to the extent of their cash investment in the property.

If there is a disagreement with a limited partner, he or she can be replaced. If a partner wants out of the transaction, he or she can sell their share of the partnership at whatever price they are willing to accept, and a buyer is willing to pay. As a general partner, you can also collect a management fee for your management services.

Cons: As the General Partner, the total asset is your responsibility. If for some reason, you get into financial trouble with the property, you are the only one a lender will look to, not the limited partners. If the property is liquidated, the limited partners get paid first out of the proceeds. You will have to make periodic financial reports to the limited partners. Tip: There are legal documents that must be prepared to create a limited partnership. If you are purchasing a single, small property, it most likely won't merit the cost of utilizing a constrained association structure.

How to Invest in Rentals with less Cash and Bad Credit

It's valid. You can benefit in rentals absent a lot of money—particularly on the off chance that you've fortified your credit score. In any case, in any event, when you need platinum-control credit, despite everything, you have an assortment of next to zero cash-down strategies that you can attract on to kick you off as a real estate investor.

The capacity to comprehend, perceive, and exploit other individuals' money is the sign of fruitful real estate investors. Why? Since they've aced the craft of how to put resources into real estate with no money of their own. For more up to date and monetarily lashed investors, this is an alluring method to get a foot in the real estate entryway without having the monetary assets and credit to do as such. Veteran investors, then again, have discovered that utilizing other individuals' money sells their accessible assets and opens their cash to contribute more, and at last, make more. If you need to figure out how to put resources into real estate with no money of your own, you are in karma. If for only that, it's conceivable to begin without investing your very own cash.

All things considered, if you don't mean to contribute your very own money, there is something different you completely need: a dependable system. The stunt is in realizing who can support you, and how to utilize them to further your potential benefit. There is no uncertainty about it: real estate investing with no money out of your pocket is conceivable. You needn't bother with interminable cash stores of your own to secure an arrangement. You simply need to realize how to put resources into properties with the perfect individuals next to you. If you need to put resources into real estate with no money of your own, here are approaches to that:

Numerous speculation bargains come to pass all through the real estate advertising on a yearly premise. The larger part is accomplished through traditional lenders and organizations like banks. However, some are practiced through less traditional means. A great extent, this is because the investor couldn't raise the capital or didn't have the credit score to do as such. It's critical to take note that while investing in real estate with no money down offers various advantages, not every single cashless arrangement is beneficial. Truth be told, investors outfitted with a wonderful credit score won't just get a more extensive cluster of options for working capital. However, they'll have more control over their money related commitments. It's to your greatest advantage as a real estate investor to guarantee that score stays first-rate, as it will give the best money sparing outlet.

There are, be that as it may, circumstances were using these options bodes well. Consider the way that cash purchasers are more straightforward than standard mortgage buys when contrasted with traditional loans, which are delayed satisfying. With cash close by, this technique can give a phenomenal high ground at the arrangement table. For an investor with neither the credit score nor the budgetary ability to buy a property through traditional means, it's imperative to recollect despite everything you have options accessible. The accompanying gives a comprehension of the numerous ways you can put resources into real estate with no money of your own:

Hard Money Lenders

In contrast to private money, hard money lenders put forward charges as focuses. Extending from three to five, these focuses speak to an additional, forthright rate expense dependent on the obtained sum; this is over the loan fees hard money lenders charge, which range somewhere in the range of 10 and 18 percent. Charges and loan fees are not general with hard/private money lenders, so investors need to do their due tirelessness.

Private Money Lenders

These loans, which carry speed and productivity to each exchange, will commonly cost investors something to the tune of six and 12 percent enthusiasm on the money obtained. The most common strategy when financing real estate manages no money down is using hard or private money lenders. These loans are not given from banks, yet rather individuals and associations anticipated financing theories for an appearance. In like manner, these loans are, generally, associated with their one of a kind games plans of criteria, which moreover join more charges and higher financing costs to manage. When utilizing these kinds of lenders, a great standard guideline is to discover homes that can be obtained for 50 pennies on the dollar.

Wholesaling

As the starting course to real estate investment, wholesaling requires neither a high credit score huge totals of cash down. Rather, it essentially comes down to having the correct numbers set up. Real estate wholesaling, at its center, comprise of finding limited properties, doling out the agreement to a potential purchaser, and getting paid to do as such.

Equity Partnerships

An extremely normal way in real estate investment is through partnerships. What one investor comes up short on, the other can make up for — and numerous partnerships will involve one accomplice finding a troubled property at a limited cost, while the other one uses their credit score and working money to fund it; simply make sure everybody is carrying something to the table. For better investors, perspectives, for example, objectives, hazard, jobs, and return, ought to consistently be talked about before making any kind of partnership.

Home Equity

An alternative option for investors with no forthright cash is home equity. This can be a suitable option since property estimations have gone up as of late, which means there could be more capital accessible than you might suspect. For investors hoping to profit by this course, there are commonly two options: revamp the principal mortgage and make money out renegotiate, or keep the main advance set up and include a home equity credit extension.

Option to Buy

Occasionally, regarded as a "rent option," this strategy enables investors to gain properties without at first taking lawful proprietorship. Be that as it may, the investor will sign a legitimate "option to purchase" from the homeowner at a cost later. In return, the investor leases the property out on a long-haul premise with an understanding set up to buy the property sometime soon for a recently set sum.

Seller Financing

In contrast to conventional loans, merchant financing works this way: the investor buys the property from the homeowner/vendor, instead of a bank, and the consent of the different sides to an arrangement that expresses a loan cost, reimbursement reschedule and results of default that the two gatherings have settled upon.

House Hacking

House hacking, as its name proposes, is a real estate procedure that grants insightful investors the capacity to exploit an extraordinary circumstance. Even more explicitly, notwithstanding, this specific leave system will observer investors win rental salary by leasing their main living place. Those with multi-unit homes, for instance, may lease the units they are not living in. That way, the lease created may help pay for the mortgage, enabling the proprietor to possibly live mortgage-free.

Then again, those in single-family homes can pick to lease rooms when they can. In any case, house hacking enables investors to all the while relieving the danger of vacancy will build an income.

Quality scores equivalent better mortgage rates, which results in long term reserve funds, and eventually ends up profiting you — the investor.

Government Loans

Government loans are maybe the most notable of the considerable number of wellsprings of financing made available to the present investors. Below is a list of the government loans you may as of now be comfortable with:

- FHA Loan
- USDA Loan
- VA Loan
- Great Neighbor Next Door Program
- Fannie Mae Or Freddie Mac
- Vitality Efficient Mortgage (EEM)
- FHA Section 203(k)
- Local American Direct Loan
- Nearby Grants and Programs

It is important, notwithstanding, that there are parts of government loans that are not consummately appropriate for rehabbing homes for a speedy benefit. VA Loans, for instance, may just be applied to each home in turn. FHA Loans, then again, will, in general, match with loan terms that are significantly longer than private and hard cash banks. Besides, almost all government loans can take a very long time to get approval, making them less alluring than pretty much every other choice on this list. Microloans As the peer-to-peer economy keeps on molding how to land investors work together, microloans will stay a suitable alternative. Issued by people, rather than banks and credit associations, microloans are one more part of peer-to-peer loaning causing it feasible for individuals to put resources into land. It is altogether workable for microloans to be issued by a solitary loan specialist or accumulated over various investors, every one of whom is relied upon to contribute a part of the aggregate sum the borrower needs. No cash or credit? No problem. For newbies looking for how to put resources into real estate with no cash down and terrible credit, the initial step is understanding your credit score. This number, which is a factual strategy for moneylenders to decide the likelihood of you paying back the cash obtained, is a basic component when obtaining financing for real estate.

Credit scores are most times always based on a rating model, which is the most popular FICO model. These results vary from 300 to 850 and ultimately determine a person's solvency. It looks a bit like this:

- Bad Credit: 300 – 600
- Poor Credit: 600 – 649
- Fair Credit: 650 – 699
- Good Credit: 700 – 749
- Excellent Credit: 750 – 850

Although the evaluation systems each credit agency differs, which are based on different factors, the well-recognized credit score calculations are based on five major factors:

- Payment History = 35 percent
- Outstanding Balances = 30 percent
- Length of Credit History = 15 percent
- Types of Accounts = 10 percent
- Credit Inquiries = 10 percent

The initial step is recognizing what your credit score is and seeing how it impacts your investment technique moving ahead. Contingent upon what your score is, you may be eligible for a traditional loan and be qualified to verify up-front payment assistance. Appreciating where you remain in the financial realm of credit will just upgrade your real estate investment procedures, just as your financing options. Finding out how to put resources into real estate with no cash down is significant as an investor; however, it's not forever your solitary option.

How to Analyze an Area for Rental

The first thing we did when we started looking for a property was to look for an area of the city, we thought would have possibilities, both quality-wise and price- wise. We found a small house that needs quite a bit of work, but the other homes on the street are very attractive and well kept. Since we are interested in this location, we need to know more about the area itself, beyond the immediate block on which the home is located. We do this before we talk to the owner. There is no point in wasting his time or our time negotiating with the owner if we discover later that the city sewage treatment plant backs up to the home. (Fortunately, it is on the south side of the property, and the prevailing winds are usually out of the north)! You'll still want to look for another property.

Drive the Neighborhood: Take a drive around the entire area. You may want to extend your tour several blocks or more from home. Observe what the entire neighborhood is like. Are there signs of deterioration throughout the area? Pay attention to traffic, schools (in case you want to sell to someone with children), shopping, police and fire protection, any major plans the city, county, or state may be planning that could affect the neighborhood, for better or worse. As an example, we had a state prison locate within a mile of a nice upper-middle-class neighborhood. The residents were not happy about it. Chances are, you can contact your local governmental agencies to see what is planned for the area you are considering. It is an affair of public record and available to anyone. It's best to find out before you buy a property and then have trouble selling it later.

Drive the Neighborhood:

Take a drive around the entire area. You may want to extend your tour several blocks or more from home. Observe what the entire neighborhood is like. Are there signs of deterioration throughout the area? Pay attention to traffic, schools (in case you want to sell to someone with children), shopping, police and fire protection, any major plans the city, county, or state may be planning that could affect the neighborhood, for better or worse. As an example, we had a state prison locate within a mile of a nice upper-middle-class neighborhood. The residents were not happy about it. Chances are, you can contact your local governmental agencies to see what is planned for the area you are considering. It is an affair of public record and available to anyone. It's best to find out before you buy a property and then have trouble selling it later.

Condition of Other Properties in the Area:

Check out individual homes for signs of general neglect. If a lot of them are in poor condition, you may want to reconsider. Example: A team listed a group of eleven small apartment complexes (all two to four units in size) on a four-block long street of similar buildings. They had control of the fourth block on the street. They found a buyer for all but two of the buildings, and he began to fix them up. They were in horrible condition but only cosmetically. The two remaining buildings just did not sell, and they were at the end of the fourth block on a cull-de- sac. I ended up buying the two remaining buildings. We called them our "slums" because that's what they were when we took over. We had control of the entire fourth block on the street of all apartment buildings. We set to work renovating them and turning them into very attractive buildings with fresh paint, clean and newly decorated interiors, and all new landscaping. Unfortunately, we could not get the owners of the first three blocks of buildings to go along with our renovation plans.

Checking the Area in General: Now that you are satisfied with the area immediately surrounding the property you want to purchase, take one final look at the total area. You may have already done so. Observe the type of properties in the area. Look for signs that the area is going downhill. Are there boarded up or rundown buildings. They may not immediately affect your property now, but they could be a sign of what is happening to the area. If the neighborhood and surrounding area look good, there is one final thing we should do before to try to buy the home. What about "for rent" signs on a lot of the buildings you may see? Quite often, a building owner will keep a "for rent" sign on a property at all times. He or she wants to have a continual stream of potential renters lined up in case he or she has a vacancy.

It is not necessarily a sign that there are a lot of vacant units in the building. If you are a night owl and want to find out how many vacant apartments are in the area, drive it at 2:00 A.M. some morning to see how many cars are in the parking lot. A good indication that the building is also fully rented is if the parking lot is full. Keep in mind that some tenants will have two automobiles. Usually, there are assigned spaces for each tenant plus guest spaces. If you are looking at a single-family home or duplex, this early morning trip is not necessary. You can also consider determining the quality of tenants who occupy the units by the automobiles in the parking lot. If the lot is filled with junk cars, you may want to keep looking for another building.

Once you are satisfied that the area is a good one, it's time to get serious about trying to buy the house you saw. At this point, you have a good idea of what prices are in the area, by calling others for sale signs and asking, and you know the area.

How to Analyze the Market

The final study you should make, before meeting with the seller to discuss a purchase, is to analyze the current and potential market conditions. No, you do not have to become a knowledgeable economist to do this. What you do need to do is get a feel for were your current market trends might be heading. Checking vacancy rates in the area was once part of the process. Are most of the rental properties pretty much fully leased or are there a sizable amount of vacancies. Your local news media and chamber of commerce often have this information available. Here are some of the facts you should know before making a purchase decision.

1. Area vacancies: How is the rental market for the type of property you are considering? If area vacancies are ten percent or more area-wide or city-wide, you may want to think twice.

2. What is the economic trend? If there are a lot of vacancies, what is the reason for them?

- Overbuilt rentals for the area. We've seen this happen, especially in office space, when every builder started putting up large office buildings, and there was suddenly a fifty percent vacancy in office properties.
- A Market turndown. If the economy is in a down cycle, this could create a lack of renters. This was also part of the cause for the high office building vacancies in the early seventies. The economy slowed down, and businesses were pulling back rather than expanding. Not only did new office space suffer from lack of prospective tenants, but

also, existing space was being vacated by businesses that could no longer afford the space.
- Poor economic news can cause a turndown in the economy. We saw what happened to the market when several large corporate entities were discovered covering up actual loses.

There is an interest thought here. I firmly believe that we are a victim of our circumstance. In other words, our own worst enemy is us. If a major economist tells us the economy is going to slump, sure enough, the market plunges the next day. If, however, the economist tells us the economic outlook is great, the market soars the next day. In truth, we always manage to pull ourselves up and turn things around.

In any event, getting back on the subject, historically, we experience slowdowns in the economy. The reason you want to take a close look at economic trends before you buy is to try and determine two things. First, is the economy in a down turning mode or going up? Second, if it is down, what is the outlook for a quick turn-around? You have an advantage in buying when the market is slow. Motivated sellers are often more plentiful, and prices are more negotiable. Taking a little time to research the market is an important step in being reasonably assured we are not in a long-term slump.

· d. We're back to legwork again. Drive various areas of the city, especially those comparable to the one you are considering. Take notes on "for rent" signs on properties. Call several of them to see what is available, how many are available, and what the rental is. Again, you can get a feel for the market conditions by seeing how many property owners have vacancies and if they are offering any rental concessions to get tenants.

Tip: Don't be fooled by rental signs on the property. This was mentioned earlier. Quite often, rental signs are left on a property to keep a flow of potential tenants on the books.

· e. Keeping Current: It is important to stay current on what is happening, especially in your city, that can affect your rentals. It is a large industry moving into town or leaving town? Is a major change expected in the area, such as a new Interstate highway, municipal improvements that will increase the flow of traffic to the area, such as a major sports stadium? Changes, such as that will affect retailers but not apartment building owners unless it will be a spring or fall training site for the national team. These people will be looking for short term rentals.

Offer and Negotiations

Negotiating for the Best Price and Terms

The term negotiation refers to a negotiation process with another person or other party to reach a mutually acceptable agreement between all parties involved. Negotiations involve the exchange of two or more items that all parties agree to consider to be of equivalent value, such as the exchange of real estate money. Learning how to become an artistic and effective negotiator is like learning another skill. With the right training, you can learn to become an expert negotiator, an expert in the successful execution of almost all real estate transactions. The more you understand the psychology of interacting with others, the more likely you are to reach a mutually acceptable agreement.

Over time, you will know that many buyers and sellers you are dealing with are amateurs, which means they do not buy or sell real estate at any frequency. Therefore, they are not skilled in the methods and techniques of a prime negotiator like the ones he could use. Fans participate in the real estate market as needed. Expert investors, on the other hand, have mastered six phases of successful trading and are using them each time to their advantage.

Steps to Successful Negotiations

- 1. Psychology 101
- 2. Market knowledge is key
- 3. The trial balloon
- 4. The blame game

- 5. The Chess Player
- 6. Put it in writing

Psychology 101

One of the necessary things to remember when negotiating with others is that you are dealing with people, many of whom develop an emotional attachment to their property somewhere along the way. Most of the buyers and sellers you deal with are not professionals and often find it difficult to separate their emotions from the rational, clear thinking that is required to conduct business. After a certain point in the sales process, people become emotionally engaged, which causes them to act in a manner they otherwise wouldn't.

This is true for both buyers and sellers. The easiest way to illustrate this technique is by using an example. Often when buyers come to one of our communities, they have already looked at several different houses in just as many communities and therefore have a difficult time making up their minds.

After all, buying a new home is one of the most substantial financial decisions a person will make in his or her entire lifetime. Since we understand that a very real emotional and psychological transition must occur in the mind of the prospective buyer, we are prepared to deal with it through a process of encouraging the buyer to take a series of baby steps. That's right—baby steps. Before a child can learn to walk, one must first become familiar with four-legged walking. Once your little body has mastered this feat, you will be ready for the next phase of your progression. Take the first step, then the second, and maybe even the third. Meanwhile, his parents, as delighted as they are, sing songs of praise and encouragement, encouraging him at every turn. After two or three months, the baby has mastered the task of "taking small steps" and sometimes starts walking quickly, which eventually becomes a race. Before you know it, it's as busy as possible everywhere, and you find yourself saying, "This kid is running out on me. I wish it slowed down long enough for me to catch my breath!

    Believe it or not, people are buying homes at a similar stage of growth. However, the main difference is that these stages of progress happen in the human psyche as opposed to the physical world. Experienced sales agents admit that very few people buy a home on the premises. This is not to say that it is not happening; it is more an exception than a rule. Buyers cite more reasons than you can imagine delaying their decision. They want to think about it or sleep, pray about it, consult with a lawyer or accountant, or ask Uncle Joe to review it. All these reasons for delaying decision making are completely legitimate in the eyes of the buyer, and if you are a salesperson, you need to be prepared to face those reasons. If this is not the case, someone else who understands the process better than you will make the sale you just lost. The key to its success is the commitment of the potential customer to take steps forward, or step by step, to make a bigger decision.

    This baby step provides the buyer with an opportunity to make a small, risk-free commitment to you. Even though he or she has not officially purchased the house, the buyer has taken an incremental step toward doing so. Taking this baby step is much more powerful than you may be inclined to think. What happens is that a transition begins to take place in the mind of the buyer. Although the buyer in this example only gave a deposit of $250, in her mind, that magnificent new home now belongs to her. A shift in her thinking has taken place.

Now, instead of trying to decide if she should buy the house, the buyer is thinking about all the positive reasons to reinforce her decision. The buyer's intellect changes from one of fear and negativity to one of rationalization and justification. She more than likely will stop looking at other houses, which is exactly what you want him or her to do.

Market Knowledge Is Key

To be successful in this business, you must have a comprehensive knowledge of the market you are dealing with. It is impossible to negotiate the best price without it. You must understand property values in your respective market as well as, or better than, the parties with whom you are doing business. You can use your market knowledge to make sound arguments to the parties you are dealing with to support the price and terms for which you are negotiating. By showing them what similar properties are selling for, you are presenting unbiased information that will enable them to feel more comfortable with the price differential.

Whether you are buying or selling vacant lots, rental houses, or apartment buildings, the need to thoroughly understand the market is the same. You can't afford to pay too much for the rental property you are interested in buying, and you can't afford to sell for too little when it comes time to sell. As a professional real estate investor, you need to be knowledgeable about the market you are trading in and have a thorough knowledge of to be completely successful. Without this crucial information, you will find it too soon to discover that you cannot survive in the real estate industry.

The Trial Balloon

The term trial balloon started with the starting of hot air balloons that at first were unmanned. The historical backdrop of tourist balloons stretches out back to 1782, when two siblings, Joseph and Etienne Montgolfier, initially started trying different things with a balloon trip close to Paris, France. Joseph had imagined the idea of utilizing balloons to enter via air the secure stronghold of Gibraltar. His goal was to utilize the balloons to convey a whole armed force directly over the leaders of the English to rapidly overcome them. In 1783 a few unmanned trial balloons were propelled to test this clever idea. At long last, on August 27, 1783, a culminated trial balloon was propelled, flying separation of roughly 12 miles. Ignorant that a wonder such as this even existed, the French workers in Geneses, where the balloon slipped from its grand flight, were overwhelmed. Expecting that some beast had tumbled from the sky, the laborers immediately assaulted the balloon with pitchforks, rendering it pointless. On September 14 of that equivalent year, another trial balloon was propelled. Instead of a man, a wicker confine containing a sheep, a chicken, and a duck was connected to the balloon to check whether they would get by in the higher environment. The flight was considered a triumph since each of the three creatures returned securely to earth, safe, however maybe somewhat shaken by their history-production flight.

In addition to the fact that the term trial balloon is yet utilized broadly today, it only from time to time alludes to a tourist balloon. The term does, in any case, share a comparative significance in that when it is utilized, it frequently alludes to a trial or a test of something.

Legislators are said to coast trial balloons all the time. For instance, a representative may have one of his clerical specialists release an idea or a story to the press about expanding the business duty to fund-raise for instructive purposes. The congressperson is as a rule endeavoring to gauge their constituents' responses to decide whether they will acknowledge or dismiss the idea. Drifting the unmanned trial balloon through a break to the press manages the representative the chance to "test the waters" without uncovering himself. If the open responds positively, the congressperson can then actually "man" the balloon and make realized his goals to increment charges. Else, he will remain securely quiet with his notoriety secure.

The trial balloon method, as it applies to land, can be a very compelling arranging instrument. Throughout your discourse with the other party, regardless of whether a purchaser or merchant, you can dispatch your very own progression trial balloons. The system works by unpretentiously skimming a suggestion every once in a while, to test what the other party might be eager to do. Through perception, you can gauge the other party's response by how he reacts to the suggestion.

You can coast a wide range of trial balloons. For instance, you can test the other party's readiness to consult on the loan cost, the upfront installment, conveying back a subsequent home loan, the date of shutting, and a large group of different things too.

The Blame Game

The blame game technique does precisely as its name suggests by redirecting blame or fault toward another path. The technique is utilized to move or move the blame from you as the speculator to some other person or thing. You presumably are considering what it is you may get blamed for when consulting with others. The appropriate response is nothing if you utilize this technique.

An essential key to effective exchanges with another gathering is to build up a constructive association with that person. You need to assemble compatibility with that person by remaining concentrated on the constructive. Utilizing this approach will manufacture their trust in you and make a climate of trust, subsequently permitting a discourse of price and terms to happen. I read various years before an arranging procedure that adopted precisely the contrary strategy. The idea was to endeavor to thrash the seller in price by reprimanding everything about his home by pointing out the entirety of its numerous faults. This approach does is affront the seller and makes him not have any desire to work with you under any conditions, paying little mind to the amount you may offer.

I'm certain you've heard the well-known adage about getting more honeybees with nectar. A similar rule remains constant concerning purchasing and selling land. The blame game technique bears you the chance to consult at an increasingly great cost or terms by moving the blame or fault to either an enliven item, for example, an outsider or a lifeless thing, for example, a venture. How about we take a gander at a model. Expect that you are strolling through the seller's home, and you see that the rug is exhausted and should be supplanted. You may state something like, "Mr. Seller, you have an extremely decent home. It's undeniable you've taken great consideration of it throughout the years.

Mr. Seller, is that something you would consider?" Can you perceive how this approach may be more powerful than legitimately criticizing the seller's home? Rather than distancing the seller, you have complimented him. The partner referenced here could be anybody. It could be a true-blue partner from your organization, or it could essentially be a mate, a companion, or a relative. It doesn't generally make a difference in what its identity is. The fact is that you are moving or moving the fault-finding to someone else who is absent. You can blame your partner for essentially anything you can consider. On the off chance that you don't care for the yard, blame your partner. If you don't care for the rooftop, blame your partner. If you don't care for paint, blame your partner. You get the idea.

Put It in Writing

This negotiating system is utilized more fittingly as an end method and more especially for merchants. The set it in motion system is to be utilized as a guarded measure against potential buyers who might glide trial balloons as a component of their technique. As a vendor of recently built homes for Symphony Homes, I have customers coast trial balloons constantly. For instance, they may express something to one of our sales agents like, "We truly like the house, yet Builder XYZ down the road is offering a free landscaping package with his homes. Can you be able to toss in a landscaping package to coordinate what he is offering?" It seems like an ordinary trial balloon skimmed by a forthcoming buyer attempting to beat us on cost. Scarcely a day passes by that we don't get an arrangement question this way. How would you figure we ought to respond to this sort of inquiry? How might you respond? In the event that the sales agent was to answer by expressing that, indeed, we would consider including a landscaping package at no additional charge, the buyer would expect that on the off chance that he purchases the house, he will get the free landscaping package. By recommending that we will think about it, we have recently surrendered a bit of our dealing power. Besides, when we concur verbally without dedication from the buyer, he will coast another trial balloon, and after that one more and again, etc. As a dealer, you can't bear to give up control of the sales procedure to the buyer.

The proper reaction by the sales agent goes something like this. "Mr. Buyer, I can see that you truly like the house. However, I know from my involvement with the builder that he won't consider any offer except if it is in writing. On the off event that you are extremely genuine about obtaining this wonderful home, and I accept that you are, at that point, let me recommend that we plunk down together and incorporate the landscaping package at no additional charge as a major aspect of your offer. A while later, I'll present the offer, alongside your sincere cash store, to the builder. I can't guarantee you that he will acknowledge it. However, we can unquestionably try it out." Can you perceive how viably this strategy can be utilized to arrange yourself directly into a deal? As opposed to giving the buyer any sign verbally that you might be adaptable, you get him to make a promise to you by expressly stating it. This tells you that the buyer is not kidding. My organization gets tire kickers consistently, a significant number of whom are out taking a gander at houses since they don't have anything better to do. My sales agents know not to offer anything endlessly through a straightforward inquiry and response exchange. Rather, they utilize the buyer's trial balloon as a chance to review the deal. If a buyer needs you to consult on cost, basically instruct him to carefully record it, and you'll be glad to think about it.

The Chess Player

The game of chess is played by two opponents who systematically move their chess pieces around the board in a key fashion and execute a progression of well-arranged moves. While being ever conscious of the opponent, the chess player cautiously puts each piece in a situation in an arrangement like fashion, hanging tight for the perfect chance to strike. Albeit each piece is moved with exact thought, the players bend over backward to contain all indications of ostensibly noticeable feeling that possibly could reveal their fundamental intentions. At that point, at the perfect moment, on recognizing an area of weakness or helplessness, the player rapidly moves the suitable piece and reports, "Checkmate!" The keen speculator realizes that consulting for investment properties is like playing a game of chess. Every single activity is executed with purposeful exactness.

You begin the game by situating your pieces, so they coordinate those of your opponent. In a bit by bit fashion, you at that point begin to systematically move your pieces into position each in turn, until finally, everything is perfect. All through the procedure, you reveal just what the other player has to know, being mindful so as not to unveil data that may profit her. Finally, when the moment is right, and you identify an area of weakness, you rapidly move into a checkmate.

How to Manage and Keep Your Property

To improve the net income of a rental property, an investor must do one of two things: increase revenue or reduce costs. The profitability of an investment property depends directly on how you manage your products and costs. In this section, we will study several methods to reduce the cost of a rental property by implementing several changes that would have an impact on the cost of the equation. Using a combination of growing income and reducing costs is a surefire way to improve the profitability of your rental property.

- 1. Pass the buck
- 2. Hire the handyman
- 3. Utilize utilities
- 4. A taxing matter
- 5. Dialing for dollars

Pass the Buck

One easy and effective way to decrease expenses and immediately begin saving $25 to $50 every month is to pass the buck. This phrase refers to shifting responsibility from one party to another. In this case, it is the rental property owner who is shifting the responsibility of the first $25 to $50 of repair expenses to the tenant. The best time to do this is at the initial signing of the lease agreement. In the repairs and maintenance section, you simply stipulate that the tenant is responsible for paying for all minor repairs that cost $50 or less, or whatever amount you deem to be appropriate. Using this approach has several advantages to the owner. First, it will save her money each month, and second, it will save her time. Although minor repairs may not cost the owner very much in terms of money, they certainly can cost her in terms of time. Imagine if you got called every time, there was a clogged sink or a stopped-up toilet. Then multiply those phone calls times 10 or 20 rental properties, and you can see where making these types of minor repairs will get old fast. Bypassing the buck to the tenant, you are also empowering the tenant to take a degree of responsibility for the premises in which he or she lives. If the tenant knows that he must repair something if he breaks it, then maybe he will be a little more careful not to break it in the first place. Most tenants won't mind a clause in the lease agreement requiring them to be responsible for the first $50 or so of minor repairs. If the tenant does balk at it, however, just explain to him that the cost of minor repairs has been factored into the monthly rent and that without the repair clause, the rent would be $50 more per month.

Hire the Handyman

When it comes to making needed repairs on a rental property, investors have three choices. They can either make the repairs themselves, pay a professional to make them, or hire a handyman. Although each method has its advantages and disadvantages, hiring a handyman to repair your rental property often makes the most sense. The chances are that you are handy with tools yourself and are likely to have tackled a few home improvements projects at one time or another. The chief advantage of making repairs yourself is the money you'll save by not having to pay someone else. If you only have one or two rental properties and have the time, then this is probably a good choice for you. On the other hand, if you own several properties, it will become increasingly difficult to keep up with all of them. Investors also should consider that if they're spending all their time repairing houses, they will have very little time left to buy and manage them. Are you in the business of buying, managing, and selling rental properties, or are you in the business of making house repairs? You and only you can decide this. The primary advantage of hiring a professional company to make repairs is the level of expertise that the company provides. An air-conditioning unit or a furnace that needs replacing, for example, warrants the services of licensed professionals who can replace the old equipment and subsequently test the new equipment to ensure proper operation. Major repairs such as this should be left to the pros and not the amateurs. On a smaller job, such as lighting the pilot light on a furnace, however, paying top dollar for a professional company hardly makes sense.

Utilize Utilities

Depending on the area in which your rental property is located, and depending on the type of unit it is, as the owner, you may be the one paying all the utility bills. It may be, for example, reasonable and customary for owners in some markets to be responsible for paying the gas, electric, water, and sewer bills. If the utility bills are left in your name for whatever reason, you can charge the expenses back to the tenant each month and get reimbursed for any costs you may have incurred. The other option is to have the tenant put the utilities in his name and be directly responsible for them. Regardless of how you do it if possible, shift the responsibility of paying the utility bills to the tenant. Since there is no incentive for tenants to conserve energy if they are not the ones paying for it, operating expenses almost always will be higher than they should be.

Tenants naturally will reason that it's okay to go to work all day long on a hot summer day and leave the thermostat set at 65 degrees so that it will be nice and cool when they return. And why shouldn't they? After all, they're not the ones paying the utility expenses; the owner is. It is becoming more and more common, especially for single-family houses, to have the tenants be responsible for paying all the utility bills. The chances are that they already are in your area. In many states, the gas and electric bills follow the tenant, but the water and sewer bills do not. This means that if a tenant fails to pay the last month's utility bill, the gas and electric companies will pursue the tenant to collect any past due amounts. The water and sewer companies, which most often are controlled by local municipalities, however, will pursue the owner to collect past due amounts. If the bill is not paid, they may even attach a lien to the property so that when it is eventually sold, any outstanding balances along with late penalties and interest will be collected.

If this is the case in your area, you can take precautionary measures by agreeing to retain the tenant's deposit on vacating until they provide evidence that the final water and sewer bills have been paid. All the tenant needs to do is simply provide you with a receipt showing that the account has been paid in full to be entitled to a refund of her deposit. Once again, if the rental property you own is a single-family house, the chances are that the tenant is already paying for the utilities. On the other hand, if your rental property is an older multifamily property such as a duplex, triplex, or four-plex, there's a good chance that it may be master metered. Properties that are master metered are typical "all bills paid," meaning that the tenant does not pay any of the utility bills and that the owner is responsible for them. Converting a property from master metered to sub metered is easy to do. There are, in fact, companies that specialize in providing utility services such as this that have their licensed electricians and can retrofit almost any property with a turnkey submetering system. The sooner you convert your property, the sooner you'll begin reducing operating costs by a significant margin. To get existing tenants to buy into the program, you may have to reduce their rents slightly, but you'll still come out ahead.

A Taxing Matter

Property taxes represent a large portion of the operating expenses on any rental unit. Reducing the tax liability by even 5 or 10 percent can mean significant savings to the owner. Reducing a $3000 tax liability by 10 percent, for example, would yield an annual savings of $300, or $25 per month. I am not sure about you, but I prefer to keep as much of my money as possible rather than giving it to Uncle Sam. Reducing the tax liability on an investment property is not always easy, but it can be done. It can be done with little to no effort by the investor. Real estate property values are reassessed periodically for one reason or another, but most often when a property is transferred from one individual or party to another, usually triggered by a sale. If the owner of the real estate believes that the newly assessed value is too high and is out of line with the market, she may file a notice of protest. The owner will be granted a hearing, at which time she may present evidence as to why the new tax value is too high. The tax assessor or treasurer can accept the owner's claim, reject the owner's claim, or do anything in between.

If you don't want to file the protest personally, many companies specialize in representing property owners in tax protests. These companies are very familiar with the laws and corresponding market values and often know the best approach to use to reduce the assessed value. Most companies that provide this type of service only charge the client if they are successful in reducing his taxes. This fully gives them a strong incentive to represent the client because the only way they get paid is if they win the case. Fees typically are charged as a percentage of the total the client saves on his taxes for a given period.

Dialing for Dollars

One of the easiest ways to save money on a rental property is by doing what I refer to as "dialing for dollars." This simply means to get on the telephone and start calling around to do some comparison shopping. People do comparison shopping every day when they compare grocery prices from one store to the next or gas prices from station to station. Talk about a commodity that is price sensitive. Gas stations across the country vividly display the price per gallon of gasoline. Moreover, as consumers, we tend to drive an extra mile or two and sometimes more just because we know the price of gas is 3 cents cheaper at a station. If we are willing to go out of our way to save 50 cents on a tank of gas, don't you think that it makes sense to comparison shop for your rental property by calling different trades, vendors, and suppliers? Of course, it does. As a builder of new homes, I am on the phone negotiating for the best price and terms from my trades and suppliers. Building a house involves many different labor trades and various materials that must be managed throughout the entire construction phase. If I am not careful to control costs, the house will go over budget and thus reduce my company's profit margin. Price variances are scrutinized and must be explained fully so that they don't recur.

Building Your Team

There's a big difference between doing something alone and having a team. When you begin your investment career, you're probably not going to have a lot of money to hire people. As you build your investments, however, your team becomes crucial. Although real estate is property, it's all about people. There are many benefits—and sometimes a few drawbacks—to tapping into professional expertise along every step of your real estate journey. Let us discuss these, starting with a brief overview of the team you'll soon be starting to assemble for yourself.

The Infield: Your "Office"

Your in-house team comprises those professionals who'll help you deal with deals—your money people:

- Scouts
- Real estate brokers
- Mortgage brokers
- Lenders
- Bankers
- Attorneys
- Engineers
- Appraisers
- CPAs
- Bookkeepers

The Outfield: In the Market

Once you've got investment properties under your wing, you're going to need people to help you take care of them. These include the following:

- • Supers

- • Maintenance staff
- • Plumbers
- • Electricians
- • Pest control experts
- • General contractors
- • Management companies

The Finders

There's no substitute for pounding the pavement of your niche neighborhood yourself, in person, seeing and hearing its culture and ambiance, talking to its people, sampling its cuisine, perusing the notices posted on community bulletin boards, attending its events and open houses—being there. You'll never get so advanced in your real estate career that being there doesn't matter anymore. But you can't be everywhere, and, you can't always be where the deals are right when you need to be. That's why your team needs finders— people who can sniff out the deals for you.

Scouts

You need to use scouts (also called bird dogs) to help you locate great properties and hot deals. What's a scout, you ask? It's an informal, self-bestowed designation, for starters, you don't go to college and major in Real Estate Scouting. Scouts are the people on the scene, on the streets, hanging out in the neighborhood with an eye toward deals. You'll see them sitting on the front steps, and the park benches with the older retired folks, passing a beer back and forth. Talking. Listening. Finding out who's who; who's moving, who's dying, who's having a baby, who's getting a divorce or a new job. Scouts are usually young, aggressive, and hungry. They don't have the resources to do the investing themselves, but they want to be in on the action, and they'll do what it takes to find you the deal you want. If a property is about to go on the market—or if there's the slightest chance it might go on the market soon—a scout will be all over it. If Johnny Junior is the owner of the record, but he'll only sell after Johnny Senior approves—your scout will know that, too. He'll know the discount deals, the bargain deals, the hidden deals, the potential deals. All of 'me.

How do you find a scout? You don't. Scouts find you. They want your patronage, and the instant they sense you're in the market for opportunities, they'll seek you out. They'll see you in the neighborhood or (more often) at real estate meetings, clubs, seminars, breakfasts, and other events. They'll hand you a business card—which will say "consultant" or "adviser" or "analyst," by the way, and not "broker." Scouts are wheelers and dealers, and they don't want the limitations that come with trying to operate under a brokerage umbrella. And by the way, scouts will wheel and deal with you, too, when it comes to getting paid for their services. This is often done as a percentage of the deal price or as a flat fee—but there's no set fee, no set percentage, no set procedure to follow. So, negotiate. Wheel and deal with yourself.

Real Estate Broker

Why is broker selection so important? In your first year as a real estate agent, you'll have a ton of questions, uncertainties, and getting-your-feet-wet experiences. You will need to select a real estate broker who will be there with you through each step of the way. When you're first starting, you won't have the funds to compete with the big real estate brokerages when it comes to marketing, lead generation, and conversion. You'll need a broker's help getting your name out there.

A perfect real estate broker is like a director of the orchestra in nature. Both facilitate with various players to transform an innovative exchange into the real world. The job of the operator changes at the various phases of this procedure. Some of the time, he goes about as a sales rep, some of the time a purchaser's backer, frequently as an investigator, business supervisor, arbitrator, consultant, advertiser, and so forth. Aside from these, they assume numerous different jobs to facilitate the errand of their customers. At any point, you are in search of an effective specialist, you ought to see whether he has a few attributes or abilities.

Information: The best agents will consistently stay up with the latest on the most recent market patterns and procedures. The nearby market will assist him in giving better support to your customers.

System associations: Successful realtors have a wide system of contacts inside the market they serve. These associations must incorporate other realtors in their region or neighborhood, specialists, potential purchasers and sellers, appraisers, home controllers, contract advance officials, and so on. A proficient representative will consistently continue instructing himself all through his vocation.

Local housing market: An established agent always appreciates and utilizes the nuances that make a specific community's hosting market and pricing strategies as well. His focus ought to consistently remain on the nearby land showcase, which enables him to set up his disparities from his rivals.

Detail data: A great agent ought to consistently consider each detail of your property. He should direct his examination on the property in a composed way assembling all the significant data and speaking with a few sources.

Connecting with character: The agent ought to have a satisfying character that can persuade the two gatherings. From the outset, it is the character that you would see about him at your first gathering.

Enthusiasm for houses and architecture: The operator ought to have an enthusiasm for this field of land. At the point when you are conversing with him, you can discover the impression of his enthusiasm for his discussion. Intrigue drives one to information. Along these lines, a gigantically intrigued individual will have information in support of him.

The Mortgage Broker

The mortgage broker is the one who finds your money tree. He/she does the legwork—going to the lenders, getting their specifics, making the comparisons, making recommendations. In return, she receives a fee of 1 to 2 points.

I highly recommend using mortgage brokers. As a real estate investor, you've got a lot on your plate; you just don't have time to go to every bank, every financier. A good broker, on the other hand, already has the connections, the knowledge, and the smarts to find you exactly the program you need. If you're looking at a million-dollar property and hoping to put 10 percent down, for instance, a good broker will tell you right off not to waste your time talking to Citibank or Washington Mutual (for example); these banks aren't interested in 10 percent deals. A good broker will instead steer you to other institutions—may be smaller banks in Florida or California— that would love your business. A really good broker will already have close working relationships with individual bankers she can introduce you to. All of this is what he's paid for, and in my opinion, it's worth it. By the way, most brokers are paid by the bank, not you. Even if you must pay him yourself, though, do it, and be generous.

Team building doesn't stop once you've assembled your team. It goes on throughout your career. Those who take care of you, you need to take care of them. You've got a Rolodex full of service providers—so stay in touch with them. Check-in now and then, whether that's via phone call, e-mail, newsletter, birthday card, what have you. Remind them of who you are and what you're doing. Even more important, remind yourself of who they are and what they're up to. You want to know that everyone you depend on will return your calls when you're in a pinch. Keep in touch, give some attention to your team members, and they'll be receptive and ready to help you when it matters most. Just as important: Pay them well. Don't be stingy. You specialize in what you do best, let them specialize in their jobs, and let them know you appreciate it.

Attorney

If you own rental property, I am sure that you will need the services of an attorney at a point in time. Typically, you want to meet with an attorney, in the beginning, to be certain your company is set up properly, and then have him or her on call to assist in legal matters. You may even want to look for a real estate attorney who specializes in evictions.

It is only smart that you establish a relationship with a real estate attorney in advance of running into problems. Oftentimes, you will find you can pay an attorney for an hour or two of consultation time. If you ask, you may find out that, for example, a group of attorneys is holding workshops nearby or speaking to a group of investors. I know that the local attorneys in my area speak at many different meetings that I attend. If you find and join a local property owners' group, I can almost guarantee that the group will have an attorney speak at least once during the year.

Taxes, Licenses, and Insurance

If you set your rental property up like a business, in the beginning, it will keep you on track as your build on your portfolio of properties. You have income and expenses that must be accounted for and tracked, not only for your benefit but also for your state and federal taxes. You need to calculate your income, less your expenses, to determine whether you have a profit and how much in taxes may be due. (If you have a loss, you should be able to apply it against your income.) Remember that owning investment property provides opportunities and great tax benefits. One of the advantages is your ability to deduct all operating expenses and depreciation from your income while the value of your investment appreciates over time.

That said, tax laws are much more complicated for an investment property than for a personal residence. The taxation laws are quite different and change often, making it difficult to keep up. For this reason, an important part of owning property is having a great financial planner and a certified public accountant (CPA), both of whom have a great deal of knowledge in real estate.

You want to have a general understanding of the taxes and what is expected, as well as knowledge of different types of insurance available to cover your worst-case scenario. Also, you need to be sure you're complying with your local government agencies. Some cities or counties require special permits and annual inspections by the city inspector or fire department for health and safety violations.

In the tax world, there are generally two types of income: ordinary income and capital gains. Ordinary income includes your wages, salaries, bonuses, commissions, dividends, rental income, and interest income. This is taxed at varying rates, depending on your tax bracket. On the other hand, you must handle the other type of tax, capital gains, delicately, because this is the tax for income that is generated when possessions such as real estate and stock have been sold for a profit. Formulas are placed for everything regarding ordinary income and capital gains income. You need to be sure you have good records and keep your paperwork organized so that you are ready when you meet with your accountant.

New tax laws and depreciation schedules change often, and there is no way for you to keep up with everything — nor are you expected to. Find a time to schedule an appointment for a financial and tax review. Plan and be prepared. Get a tax strategy in place to help you decide when to improve your property and when to sell your investment.

Types of taxes

There are many different types of taxes. There are state and federal taxes, local taxes, in some places, city or county taxes, property taxes, and those lovely business taxes. Consult with your accountant for details, and be sure to check with your city, county, and state to be certain you are complying with all requirements.

State tax

Some states don't have a state tax, which means you're not required to do a state tax return. Investigate from the state government where your property is situated to find out about its taxes. Your accountant may have an office in that state or may have a recommendation of whom to contact to obtain the latest information. Most states have a revenue tax and/or a transfer tax, and that accounts for a large of state real estate taxes. When you do your tax return and are in a state that has this type of taxation, your accountant can prepare a form that displays the gross and net revenue produced by the properties you own and calculate what is due.

Some states impose licensing fees for property owners, like a business license due annually based on the size of your property or the income your properties generate. States may also impose licensing fees for rental property. However, the most common tax comes in the form of an amount based on the income — gross (total), not net (after expenses) — that you've generated.

Federal tax Federal taxes affect everyone. You are required to file your federal tax return on an annual basis and account for your investment property income and expenses. You may have to pay income tax on net revenue, and that amount may be different from what your friend is paying, based on the structure of your business and the way you have taken possession of your property. There are many ways to structure the set-up of your properties. You can have a partnership, a corporation, an LLC, trust, etc. A good accountant will advise you based on your situation. For instance, if your rental property is operated as a corporation, your accountant may advise you not that at the end of each year, you should not have any income in your account to avoid paying a high rate of corporate tax. (You don't want your corporation to be double taxed.) You can withdraw the money as income, spend it on improvements to your building, or pay bills. Your accountant knows what is best for your business.

Property tax

Property tax is usually ad valorem (imposed at a percentage of the value) that an owner of real estate or other property pays on the value of the property. A few state taxes are based on the size and use of the land. The taxing authority performs or requires an appraisal of the value of the property, and the tax is assessed in proportion to that value. A major segment of local and governmental agencies receives a large portion of their operating funds by taxing real estate within their jurisdiction. In many circumstances, the property tax increases quite frequently through several special assessment charges based on improvements, voted-in measures, schools, or emergency services. These charges can be a percentage or a flat rate, depending on how it was voted in by the people or governmental agency.

A professional appraiser usually assesses the property at the time you purchase the property. This is to determine the value based on the property and other comparable properties in the area. There are three basic methods of determining the fair market value of a property: the sales comparison, the cost approach, and the income approach. Both appraisers and tax assessors usually use more than one of the above approaches to be sure the final estimate of value is correct. Keep in mind that building and land are appraised separately. Most states have systems in place in which a property is reassessed or revalued periodically. Then, the higher your property is valued, the higher the property tax. Property taxes in most states are typically paid twice a year.

Property tax is a large, fixed expense. Even though taxes aren't billed monthly, you should account for them when you are doing your monthly budgeting. Some owners have the insurance and taxes inserted in their mortgage each month. This is known as an impound/escrow account and is one way to ensure you have the money for these large sums of money due twice per year. Don't be late with your property tax payments, as the penalties are usually around 10 percent. Several states allow you to charge the installments on a credit card at no additional charge, and if you have a special credit card where you accumulate points or airline mileage each month based on your charges, your points can add up quickly if you pay your property taxes this way. Many lenders address non-payment of property tax within the loan paperwork and can recall your loan, making it due and payable immediately if you don't pay your taxes. Some localities also have personal property taxes. So, if you leave a refrigerator, washer/dryer, or other furniture and fixtures in the property, you will have to report these as well. Usually, the best source is to contact the city or county government for a full list of taxes assessed or ask your accountant.

<u>Transfer tax</u>

This tax is usually levied at the time of a property sale. It is usually charged by the city, and the rate varies in each area. This amount is usually taken out and accounted for in the escrow process of purchasing or selling any property

Depreciation

In calculating your income tax obligation each year, the government allows rental property owners to take a deduction for depreciation. Understand that depreciation is not an out-of-pocket expense you incur. Rather, it is an accounting concept that allows you to deduct normal wear and tear and is a way to shelter income. This is designed to not only help with normal wear and tear but also provide you more cash flow. And it doesn't have to do with the way your building is showing its wear and tear.

Rates of depreciation vary with the class and life expectancy of the asset. For example, a building is depreciated over a long period, while a computer is depreciated over only a few years. There are limits set by law as to how long the life expectancy for certain items is. Do not decide or guess by yourself how long the asset should last. Talk to your accountant.

Repairs versus renovations

The general rule is that repair expenses are tax-deductible in the year spent, while renovation expenses are spread out over years. In other words, larger items must be depreciated over years, while the smaller items can be fully deducted immediately from that year's tax return.

Passive versus active

It is important to know the difference from the IRS standpoint and for your tax purposes. If you are in the business of real estate and it is your primary career, there are no real restrictions on the dollar amount of losses you can claim and apply against your earnings. Most people consider their rental property as an optional profession. If so, the IRS has a limit of $25,000 on yearly loss deductions. As a rule, if you are what some allude to as a quiet accomplice, you are a latent investor. As an aloof investor, you can utilize the deterioration reasoning to balance any benefit from your property. You are, by IRS guidelines, effectively engaged with the basic leadership of your investment property, regardless of whether you have an expert administration organization set up.

If you are helping with settling on choices seeing such things as significant fixes, last determination of your inhabitants, or rental sums, you are viewed as an active investor. There are many creative ways to ensure you are getting all the advantages and full write-offs available through your knowledgeable accountant.

Business licenses and permits

Building permit fees are a very popular tax with the city government. The charge is usually based on a percentage of the total improvement costs for the new construction.

Business licenses are evolving to become more popular as a requirement for rental properties. In some cities or counties, you need to have a business license for each property you own. They calculate the number of units and the income generated and charge you either a flat rate per unit or a percentage. This amount is generally due annually. Check with your local city or county offices.

Insurance If you rent out the property, you need a landlord's insurance policy. Often, ordinary homeowner's insurance doesn't cover rental property, even if your residence is in the same building. You have a substantial investment in the property you rent to others as a landlord and little control over the physical damage that can happen to it. You need to have high-quality rental property insurance featuring protection against fire, vandalism liability, and most other physical losses. Not only do you need to have insurance against these losses, but you also need to be concerned about lawsuits and having the proper insurance to cover you to defend yourself and protect your assets.

You must maintain an enough insurance that will cover them if anything happens to the rental property. An owner who is not adequately protected can face catastrophic financial problems. Insurance is one of the three major expenses you have as a rental property owner, along with your mortgage and taxes. Like taxes, insurance is one of your major fixed expenses and is something you must have. You have an option to pay the insurance along with your mortgage in the same way as your taxes, with what is called you impound or escrow account. The amount of the annual insurance is calculated monthly, and you pay that amount when you pay your mortgage each month.

Keep in mind that different insurance carriers offer different types of coverages. You need to shop around or hire an insurance agent who will shop around for you. The agent should take the time to explain the coverage and each detail, so you know the advantages and disadvantages. Be sure to factor in coverage for loss of rental income if your property can no longer be occupied due to a covered loss. For instance, if a pipe breaks and causes so much damage that your tenant must move out for the repairs to be completed, you want that lost revenue reimbursed to you by the insurance company. Also, purchase additional coverage for furnishings and appliances that are located at the residence. Your personal property will be insured for the direct physical loss caused by any of the perils (fire, flood) listed in your policy.

Types of insurance

Getting insurance is similarly as significant as getting a decent loan, and you need the correct inclusion for your circumstance, something a decent insurance operator can enable you to choose. At the point when you make sense of what inclusion you need to fulfill and agree to your lender, look around. Ensure that you're contrasting one type with its logical counterpart; for instance, be certain that the deductibles are no different when looking at arrangements.

Fire and liability

Most lenders expect you to convey both fire and liability insurance for your investment property, as this is their security net. The insurance is intended to ensure both you and the lender in case of an unexpected event. On the off chance that there is a fire in your property, you need the capacity to revamp and reestablish your property as near the first condition as could be expected under the circumstances. Indeed, even a little fire can be very exorbitant. Be certain you have liability inclusion just as substitution inclusion. Liability and fire insurance is an unquestionable requirement.

Umbrella Coverage

Insurance is likewise referred to as cover inclusion. It is a very financially savvy approach to diminish your hazard, and it is intended to enhance your different strategies. On the off chance that you were engaged with an enormous claim that was well beyond your inclusion sum, the umbrella arrangement would kick in as optional insurance and your reinforcement. This is additionally utilized by proprietors of apartment suites who can't be secured by the standard fire insurance. In that circumstance, you should cover yourself for obligation, regardless of whether the property holder's affiliation covers the fire insurance.

Flood insurance

Insurance is required by a bigger number of individuals than you may suspect. Insurance organizations sell this inclusion independently from your other insurance and are viewed as a rider arrangement. Ask whether your property is in a flood plain at the time you buy your property (this data is generally revealed during this time). Most banks require flood insurance if it is resolved that your property is situated on a flood plain.

Non-owner auto liability

This insurance is a reasonable approach that will cover you if somebody working for you is driving. This inclusion shields you from risk for mishaps and wounds brought about by the representative while working and utilizing their very own car.

Natural disaster insurance

Tremor, wind, hail, and sea tempest insurance is another thing that is sold independently as a rider to your ebb and flow arrangement. This insurance isn't required in all regions and is discretionary. Seismic tremor insurance is costly and, often, has a huge deductible.

Mortgage insurance

This is an insurance that satisfies the equalization of your mortgage if you can't make the installments for reasons, for example, a handicap or passing.

Workers' Compensation

This insurance is vital on the off chance that you have any employees, even impermanent ones. It is to ensure you if a mishap happens in the exhibition of support or expert assignment identified with your property, as you could be subject to the individual's doctor's visit expenses and loss of wages. This arrangement secures yours on location director (on the off chance that you have one) and any workers who are on the property. You may figure you don't have any employees for your investment properties; however, according to the law, you do. That unlicensed and uninsured jack of all trades or a companion who takes a shot at your property and gets installment is, in fact, a representative. Workers incorporate the occupant who is demonstrating your empty unit. If you are procuring authorized workers, confirm they are conveying their very own laborer's remuneration strategy for their employees.

Building ordinance coverage

This is a significant coverage, as it will secure you in the occasion your investment property is in part or demolished. It takes care of the expense of destruction and tidies up; alongside the expanded costs you will acquire if the property needs to meet new or stricter building code prerequisites.

Renter's protection

This is protection paid for by your inhabitants. It is essential to incorporate into your tenant contract a clarification to your occupants that their assets aren't secured by your arrangement. Most occupants have the mixed-up impression that a proprietor's protection gives coverage to the inhabitant's things. Renter's protection often covers misfortunes of the occupants' close to home assets because of fire, burglary, water harm, or different misfortune. It additionally gives security against cases made by harmed visitors. Make certain to illuminate your occupants; they aren't secured by your methodology and support (or anticipate) them to get their assurance. Explain the benefits of this incorporation and that it is commonly moderate.

Exit Strategy

The genuinely goal-oriented, especially in the field of private redevelopment, perceive the importance of a proficient business model. Building up a demonstrated framework, a plan maybe can move any business to the cutting edge of its industry. In like manner, both money related additions and self-awareness may exponentially increment within sight of a well-formulated strategy. The significance of a real estate exit strategy is, subsequently, never to be thought little of. The individuals who set aside the effort to acquaint themselves with the complexities of every technique might be remunerated as needs are. On the other hand, the individuals who disregard to recognize the advantages of a fitting Real estate exit strategy might be voided of the chance to accomplish importance in their industry. In the expressions of Alan Liken, "Neglecting to plan is planning to fizzle." Ultimately, it is dependent upon the individual investor to decide their success, comparative with their companions. Notwithstanding, executing one of various well-contrived Real estate exit strategies will without a doubt, give anybody a noteworthy preferred position over their rivals.

What Is A Business Exit Strategy?

A business exit strategy is a businessperson's plan to either sell or move ownership in an organization. An exit strategy is what it seems like: an exit plan. Business owners can utilize it to either make a benefit or to confine misfortunes when fundamental. Business owners commonly consider potential exit strategies before consistently starting a new business. The motivation behind this is because not exclusively exit plans give an exit from the organization. They additionally serve to direct business choices end route. There isn't one right answer about planning a business exit strategy. Some business owners will pick to offer offers to a current accomplice, while others like to just close the business at one point in time. An ideal exit will rely upon the size of the organization, the owners' course of events, and budgetary objectives, and the sky is the limit from there. Get the job done to say: picking the correct business exit strategy takes a cautious idea. In any case, when planned effectively, it can fill in as an ultimate objective and help for business owners.

What Is A Real Estate Exit Strategy?

Real estate exit strategies are plans in which the investor expects to expel oneself from a land deal. The choice to execute a sound exit strategy is urgent to success, as the right approach will guarantee boosted benefits and insignificant dangers. Very regularly, investors neglect to understand the importance of instructing themselves on legitimate Real estate exit strategies. Accordingly, we have set aside the effort to give similarly invested people a manual for a few exit strategies. Our objective in making this framework is to furnish you with the data expected to settle on well-in-shaped choices when picking the correct exit strategies for your deals.

An exit strategy is significant because it not just aides an investor's choices all through a given deal, yet also, directs how they will amplify the productivity. While the speed of execution is critical when endeavoring to encourage exchange, don't endeavor to start a deal without assessing potential exit strategies. As an investor, it is basic to assess every situation given the end. That is, have a plan for each house before you buy it.

Investors ought to have a reasonable comprehension of how they plan to benefit from each land venture before they even meet with an imminent vender. Acquainting yourself with every individual Real estate exit strategy can spare your business a huge number of dollars, if not millions, over a whole profession. It is never astute to deliberately go into exchanges with a dealer without knowing how you will be exiting from the deal. Not exclusively will visually impaired desire increment dangers. However, it will destroy any potential opportunity to consult from a place of intensity. Fail to consider an exit strategy decreases potential benefits all the while was expanding dangers.

How to Choose the Right Exit Strategy

The decision regarding which real estate investing strategies to use is not as rudimentary as it may appear. There are several key factors to take into consideration when planning an exit strategy. At last, the potential benefit of each deal is associated with the separate strategy that is picked. Seeing each plan will enable each investor to boost returns on their speculation. Lamentably, there is no brilliant standard that separates every strategy for specific situations. In this manner, knowing which Real estate exit strategy to utilize is reliant on the investor's recognition with the following variables:

- Short and long-term goals
- Experience level
- Time to close
- Purchase price
- Terms
- Property value
- Condition of the property

- Market conditions
- Supply and demand
- Financing options
- Potential profitability
- Location of the property

Real Estate Strategies

- Wholesaling
- Flipping
- Buy and Hold Real Estate
- Seller Financing
- Lease Options
- Rehabbing
- Bank Owned Homes
- Traditional

Real estate strategies directly correspond to the individual following upon them. Investors are required to depict between every choice dependent on their ideal result. The exit strategy they pick relies upon the measure of money they need to put resources into the task and their degree of experience. It is critical to take note that there is no set in the stone strategy. Be that as it may, knowing most of the various approaches to exit from a deal can build productivity, as you will realize how to explore even the most negligible of deals. The following is a run-down of real estate exit strategies you might consider in the future:

Wholesaling

A discount arrangement will observer the investor go about as the mediator between a seller and an end buyer. The investor will discover and rapidly sell a property for a decent net revenue. There are two strategies in which an investor can discount: They can either sell or "appoint" their buy agreement to an end buyer, or they close on the property and quickly resell the property to another investor as a "twofold close." Wholesalers regularly don't contribute individual funding to encourage bargains and will charge a wholesaling expense. These elements make wholesaling an alluring method to begin in real estate contributing.

Flipping

Rehabbing, additionally ordinarily called house flipping, takes into consideration the biggest of overall revenues, as it enables an investor to sell the objective property at full market esteem. A recovery includes acquiring a house, revamping it, and selling it for more than the first venture costs (price tag and fix costs). The equation for an effective flip arrangement incorporates finding a property at under market an incentive in a market where a request is solid, assembling a dependable group of temporary workers, adhering to the recovery spending plan and course of events, and after that at last, selling the property rapidly to the most noteworthy offer conceivable. Notwithstanding, because different variables can go amiss, flipping has some related hazard to consider.

Buy and Hold Real Estate

Buy and hold real estate is a comparative idea to that of rehabbing. In any case, rather than selling the revamped property, an investor rents it out to get month to month income. This choice is unique about just buying a property at the market worth and transforming it into an investment property, on account of the rehabbing that is included as an additional progression. Obtaining a property at an extraordinary cost, and after that boosting its quality and appearance with certain fixes and remodel won't just improve the property estimation (and in this way the arrival on your speculation), it will enable you to expand the rental rates. This is a prevalent real estate exit strategy for those hoping to develop value in a benefit. Be that as it may, ensure that you are prepared to assume the obligations of property the board.

Seller Financing

As its name recommends, the seller financing system includes an inventive strategy that allows the owner to offer the property to a purchaser. The owner funds the arrangement and goes about as a bank. Be that as it may, monthly payments are granted to the owner. The seller keeps up the home loan credit to cover the business cost. This kind of game plan gives greater adaptability to both the purchaser and the seller, instead of financing through a lender. On the off chance that you are acquiring property, seller financing can enable you to purchase more properties, doesn't influence your credit report, and gives a swifter shutting process. Likewise, you might have the option to bring putting practically zero down for an up-front installment. As the seller, enabling purchasers to fund the purchase through you enables your postings to hang out in the market. Seller financing can likewise make a wellspring of monthly salary – may be at an incredible loan cost – and spread out assessment necessities also.

Lease Options

A lease option, also called rent-to-own, enables the owner to lease the property to a tenant, however, with the option to purchase it sometime in the future. Regularly, the owner and tenant will concur upon a rental period, after which the tenant will have the option of acquiring the property from the owner. When the rental time frame closes, and the tenant chooses to push ahead with the purchase, their monthly payments will at that point be made towards the purchase of the property. These payments won't be not at all like making contract payments yet are made to the owner rather than a lender.

Rehabbing

Rehabbing is a hybrid combination of rehab and wholesale. During the preparation phase, minimal work is done to help the property achieve sales quality, so this is a great option for investors who want to do some DIY without a full commitment in Facility A with fixed arrangements. Here are some examples of ways to prepare: Give a new job to paint the interior and exterior, update the landscape, and maybe replace the carpet. Escort sessions do not have to be overly expensive or difficult and are usually limited to activities that can be done without the help of professionals. However, the time, energy, and money invested in the preparation phase depend entirely on the investor. They are often sold to rehabilitated people who will continue to repair it.

Houses belonging to the bank

A bank-owned or property-owned house is a property sold by a credit institution, such as a bank. When the property is seized, the financial entity returns it and sells it to a new customer at market value. Because maintaining and maintaining these assets is expensive for banks, they are interested in selling them as quickly as possible. To do this, they generally remove all the estate assets and debts. Bank-owned homes are for sale through real estate auctions or through the lender's special site, which houses REO. Learning how to navigate the real estate auction process is, while not your standard exit strategy, learning how to navigate real estate auctions can create a good business.

Traditional

The traditional exit strategy is to simply buy a property and then hire a real estate agent to sell it at a higher price. Investors who rely on this strategy will generally finance the property themselves or work with a mortgage lender. The traditional exit strategy is attractive because of its simplicity; however, investors who do not buy at a low price may face high holding costs and low-profit margins. The profitability of the purchase agreement with depends entirely on the purchase price of the house; without complete remediation, investors can only sell the property. Therefore, to successfully implement the traditional exit strategy, investors must ensure the best possible purchase price. Investors interested in buying and selling should explore motivated sellers, high-performance markets and commercial techniques.

Real estate avoidance strategy mistakes to avoid

While investing in real estate is a good opportunity to make a lot of money and achieve the lifestyle you want, there are risks that every investor should consider. More specifically, some factors may prevent or even ruin a proposed real estate exit strategy. The following factors can destroy any potential exit strategy:

• Problems with tenants causing loss of income

• A clear absence of a claim, a blocked deposit, or the withdrawal of a lender may prevent the return of the property.

• Unexpected maintenance costs can deny benefits

- Mismanagement of assets can diminish the value and impair potential cash flow.
- Depreciation

Understanding the factors that can prevent most real estate exit strategies from working is crucial for any investor. However, smart investors neutralize potential obstacles with multiple strategies. A backup plan is important because things can change at any time. A plethora of exit real estate strategies will reduce immediate risks and allow investors to increase their return on investment. Due to their lack of experience, relatively new investors in the industry should stick to projects that include exit strategies that they are familiar with. New investors should always start with projects that require minimal work. As they gain experience, they can begin undertaking larger projects that require more complex and perhaps more cost-effective exit strategies. But until then, it's always good to know that you can always switch to the most advanced strategies when you have some experience under your belt. Answer the question in this way, and it will be placed in the most favorable position possible.

The Importance of Record Keeping

Keeping precise records is imperative to guarantee your monetary success and to keep IRS cheerful. You can start by setting up a basic accounting framework utilizing Quicken or one of the other well-known PC programs. You can set up records to account for each income and expense item you will incur in the operation of your property. These include:

- Income Received
- Income from Rents
- Income from Other sources, such as coin laundries
- Common Area Maintenance (CAM) charges in office buildings

Advance Rents and Security Deposits: Some states require you to keep security deposits in a separate account and pay the tenant interest on that money while you are holding it. When a tenant moves out, you do a final inspection of the unit and determine how much, if any, of the security deposit you will keep covering any damage done by the tenant. Normal wear and tear are not chargeable. Advance rents are yours to keep. The purpose is to have extra months' rent paid in advance to cover the rental if a tenant fails to pay one month or moves out unexpectedly and without notice.

Operating Expenses: Set up a separate ledger sheet for each of the operating expenses you have in the operation of the property. These can include taxes, insurance, payroll, water, electric, trash removal, repairs, and maintenance, etc. A full list is included with the forms and checklists at the end of the book. It is important to review these expenses items regularly to ensure none of them are suddenly getting out of line and, if so, why. It is used to pay the final rent payment if a tenant lives out the full term of the lease.

Mortgage Payments: You will have mortgage amortizations schedules when you close on the property. Set up ledger pages for each mortgage showing a monthly breakdown of the total mortgage payment, interest deducted and principal payment. You, or your account, will need this information at tax time. If you also keep you abreast of how far your mortgage principal balances are being reduced.

You will want a section set up for your costs on the property. This includes your acquisition costs, renovation costs, and closing costs.

Although it is probably not necessary as part of your accounting records, you need to set up a record of how much value the repairs you made have. You may have only spent $2,000 out of your pocket, but having the work done for you would have cost $7,200. When the time comes to sell, this will be important, both to the IRS as well as a potential buyer. You can show the buyer how much money you spent renovating the property. (You are not lying. Your time and labor were worth something, too.) You'll also need a section to show the annual taxable depreciation you took.

During the initial period, right after you purchased the property, you may have had to carry costs to keep the property at a breakeven level. This will show up in your profit and loss statement for the end of the year reporting. Setting up a simple bookkeeping system is not difficult with the software that is available today. A few minutes a month is all that it takes to keep your records current and be able to know where you always stand.